P9-DGR-117

Food from the Radical Center

Food from the Radical Center

Healing Our Land and Communities

Gary Paul Nabhan

Washington | Covelo | London

333.95097
N115

Copyright © 2018 Gary Paul Nabhan

All rights reserved under International and Pan-American Copyright Conventions. No part of this book may be reproduced in any form or by any means without permission in writing from the publisher: Island Press, 2000 M St., NW, Suite 650, Washington, DC 20036.

ISLAND PRESS is a trademark of the Center for Resource Economics.

Library of Congress Control Number: 2018948926

All Island Press books are printed on environmentally responsible materials.

Manufactured in the United States of America
10 9 8 7 6 5 4 3 2 1

Generous support for the publication of this book was provided by Furthermore: a program of the J. M. Kaplan Fund.

Furthermore:
a program of the J.M. Kaplan Fund

Keywords: rural urban divide, restoration, diversity, natural capital, biocultural conservation, food producing capacity, gardening, farmland, fencerows, soil health, bison, sturgeon, ancient grains, agriculture

Then I heard a voice say to me, "Francesco, go and restore this sacred place, for as you can see, it has fallen into disrepair."

—St. Francis of Assisi

What needs restoring, to me, is not American nature, but "the nature of America."

—Andrew C. Revkin, in *After Preservation*

Can we continue to do the hard work of coming together in the name of both community and land? Can we even do more of it? My guess is that we can because, if we pause to listen and honestly reflect, most of us believe that community and land are both sacred, that both must be honored.

—Charles F. Wilkinson, in *Stitching the West Back Together*

How do we awaken from the dream of separateness, from an abiding sense that the chasm that exists between us cannot be reconciled? For it would seem that the gulf in our present age could not be wider between "Us" and "Them." How do we tame the status quo that lulls us into blindly accepting the things that divide us and keep us from our own holy longing for the mutuality of kinship—a sure and certain sense that we belong to each other?

—Gregory Boyle in *Barking to the Choir:*
The Power of Radical Kinship

Contents

Acknowledgments

As my tenure as a writer has advanced since my very first poem was published in response to the Cuban missile crisis, I find a certain solace in working with editors, promoters, and publishers who I have found to be true collaborators. And so my gratitude pours out to Emily Turner and Jaime Jennings and to the other fine, bright, compassionate individuals at Island Press. In a world in which the very act of publishing has become a depersonalized and increasingly top-down endeavor, independent presses are a refreshing and much-needed antidote to despair.

Early in my career as a conservationist, a number of fast friends coached me in the art of collaborative, community-based conservation and restoration. Their guidance did not necessarily keep me from making mistakes, but they encouraged me to learn from my mistakes: Tom Sheridan, Laura Monti, James Mason, Cynthia Anson, Hope Shand, Susan Kunz, Exequiel Escurra, Luther Probst, Wendy Laird, Vernon Masayesva, Melissa Nelson, Rick and Heather Knight, Dan Daggett, Courtney White, Wendy and Warner Glenn, Mandy and Jim Metzger, Makale Faber, Richard McCarthy, Curt Meine, Peter Forbes, Nathan Sayre, Ina Warren, Richard Collins, Maribel Alvarez, Chip Taylor, Peter Raven, Jonathan Mabry, Derrick Widmark, Dennis Moroney, and Mace Vaughn. I also thank my spiritual mentors for their guidance over the years: Richard Purcell, Jim Corbett, Nelson Foster, Dave Denny and

Tessa Bielecki, John Fife, Nancy Menning, Shoshanah Kay, Richard Rohr, Doug Christie, and Martin Mosko. Blessings to you all.

I visited many people and projects in the field to gain a fresh sense of where collaborative restoration was going. For soil and water work, I am indebted to Brad Lancaster, Joe Quiroga, Ron Pulliam, Valer Clark, Laura Norman, Fred Bahnson, John Wick, Caleb Weaver, Bill Zeedyk, and David Seibert. For their work with bison recovery, I am grateful to Hugh "Sunny" Fitzsimons, Kent Redford, Andy Wilkinson, and the many members of the Intertribal Bison Council. For wild food plant restoration, I am grateful to Joyce LeCompte and her multicultural camas incubator team: Patty West, Teresa DeKoker, Robin Kimmerer, DeJa Walker, Nancy Turner, and Kat Anderson. For fish recovery, I have benefited from the fine work done by Doug Duncan, Ross Timmons, Ian Park, Mark Steiger, and Jamie Bartolino. For their turkey recovery, I am proud to know Frank Reese Jr., Patrick Martins, Paula Johnson, and Glenn Drowns, as well as my fellow traveler Aubrey Krug. For their work on heirloom apples and dates, I am grateful to Kanin and Rafael Routson, Harry Polk, the Brophy and McChesney families, Eric Baard, Dan Bussey, John Bunker, Diane Flynt, Ben Watson, Tom Burford, Lee Calhoun, Jim Veteto, and Chuck and Charlotte Shelton. For work with heritage grain recovery, I thank Thom Leonard, Amadeo Rea, Glenn Roberts, David Shields, Jeff and Emma Zimmerman, Ramona and Terry Buttons, Don Guerra, Roland Chambers, Michelle Ajamian, Sally Fox, and Monica Spiller. For pollinator work, I thank Stephen Buchmann, Mrill Ingram, Ina Warren, Rodrigo Medellin, David Suro, Paul and Elizabeth Kaiser, Homero and Betty Aridjis, Mace Vaughn, Eric Mader, Chip Taylor, Laura Jackson, Claire Kreman, Steve Buckley, John Anderson, Sam Earnshaw, Joanne Baumgartner, and Francesca Claverie.

My work on these topics has been blessed by support over the decades from the MacArthur Foundation, Pew Charitable Trust, Haury Fund, Christensen Fund, W. K. Kellogg Foundation, Packard Foundation, Hewlett Foundation, Biophilia Foundation, and CS Fund.

Conservation You Can Taste

Have you ever gone out to work with others—friends, family members, neighbors, even rank strangers—to transplant a bunch of saplings of fruit trees, ones that ultimately might outlive you all? Have you done the same for berry bushes, nut-bearing palms, fruit-bearing cacti, or tufts of perennial grasses? Have you ever helped restock a stream with fish or frogs?

For me, at least, these have been moments not only when I get my hands dirty but also when my hope gets renewed.

Have *you* also felt blessed by such moments? By working to restore the earth's bounty, you surely get some grit under your fingernails and so become inoculated with the earth itself.

Did you get down on your hands and knees during that ritual of hope, that expression of faith in other life-forms? Did you do so in a place that had been damaged or even destroyed? Did you participate in this pragmatic or perhaps prayerful ritual as a way to heal wounds that have scarred the landscape?

If you answered yes to any of these questions, then you have a place in this story.

Intentionally or accidentally, you have chosen to join the ranks of an ever-broadening social movement to restore what my friend Gretel

Ehrlich once called "the remaining riches of the living world." Those riches include the enduring seeds, the rare breeds, the forgotten fruits, the elusive fish, the still-surviving game, the dutiful pollinators, the hidden microbes and worms working in our most fertile soils, and the clean waters hidden in springs and aquifers beneath our feet.

By enhancing the food-producing capacity of landscapes and waters near where you live, you may ultimately have the chance to enjoy the sensory pleasures derived from such work, what I call *a conservation you can taste.*

It is no mere abstraction. You simply feel more connected to a habitat you know personally than to a piece of rainforest halfway around the world in a place you will never see, smell, touch, or taste.

Such "up-close-and-personal" activities, whether on the ground or hip-deep in running waters, are the hallmarks of one of the largest grassroots movements ever engaged in restoring the food-producing capacity of our planet. And if communally shared food itself is considered a sacrament by most cultures, then it should not be surprising that they believe food-producing habitats also deserve our care and our prayers.

This is a movement of people from all cultures, races, classes, and walks of life who are restoring the health of American farms and ranches, streams and lakes, and forests and orchards. As ecological-restoration visionary James Aronson has written, "It is the people who carry a vision, combined with a firm determination to accomplish it, that shape tomorrow's world, and change is imminent . . . The good news is that a very wide range and surprisingly great number of activities related to the restoration of natural capital are already happening."

Because of these efforts, the diversity of foods and beverages on American tables is greater than at any time in the last century. The number of cultivated food plant varieties in the US has more than doubled in the last thirty years, growing from 9,720 in the mid-1980s to 21,640 in the mid-2010s. We also have many more nonprofits and small companies distributing heirloom plants, up from 375 nursery and seed outlets three decades ago to more than 500 today.

Many wild species formerly used as food are also being recovered, and more sustainable harvests are already allowing some of them to move back into the marketplace. While diets are narrowing and biodiversity is declining in much of the world, a powerful countertrend is moving the US toward healthier eating and diversified farmlands.

Curiously, most of these successes were not directly accomplished by our land management agencies, although particular staff members generously supported them. Nor were they achieved by big national conservation organizations based in America's cities.

Instead, they were accomplished by individuals like you and your neighbors: teachers, cider makers, home cooks, farmworkers, backyard orchardists, small-scale ranchers, chefs of independently owned restaurants, master gardeners, naturalists, and food historians.

Their efforts were helped along by grassroots alliances fostered by the likes of the American Livestock Conservancy, the National Association of Conservation Districts, Seed Savers Exchange, the Wild Farm Alliance, Chefs Collaborative, and the North American Fruit Explorers. Such groups do play critical roles in convening and backstopping the people who do the "real work" on the ground.

The diversity of people involved has everything to do with assuring that a diversity of our foods contributes to our food security. We need a broad cross-section of America's talent to revitalize our continent's food-producing capacity.

Fortunately, this talent is being rewarded. A growing number of both rural and urban "green" jobs have been generated by the groundswell of interest in nutritious, diverse foods and in the healthy landscapes and waters that produce them.

Remarkably, landscape restoration now directly employs more than 125,000 Americans and generates more than $9.5 billion in economic output yearly. These restorative activities generate a "multiplier effect" of at least 95,000 other jobs, amounting to another $15 billion of value in indirect business-to-business contracts and sales.

Steve Zwick of *Ecosystem Marketplace* believes that the "restoration economy" in North America may now be supporting more livelihoods than logging, mining, or other extractive industries such as iron and steel production.

Ironically, this global movement of "blessed unrest and blissful restoration" has emerged at the very moment when our communities and democratic traditions are facing unprecedented stresses.

Open the pages of nearly any national newspaper, listen to any radio or television newscast, or Google one of the thousands of podcasts and blogs about current events, and you will be exposed to a plethora of reports that illustrate the acrimony emerging at nearly every level of our society. And yet, the movement for biocultural restoration is one that unites rather than divides, that sews together frayed fragments and brings forward the best of what it means to be human.

While the subject of this story is what we may call *biocultural, eco-culinary,* or *reciprocal restoration,* it is quite often enabled through a social process that has been called either *community-based restoration, collaborative conservation,* or *cooperative collaboration.*

Have you ever worked hand in hand on the land with others and discovered that you shared common values, beliefs, or goals? Did your collaboration incidentally contribute to healing old wounds in your own community? Then you yourself have reaped the benefits of collaborative conservation.

Despite social pressures to do otherwise, many of you have found common ground with others different from yourselves. Together, you have performed courageous acts of co-creation, collaborating not only with other humans but also with other species, like soil microbes, earthworms, deep-rooted plants, insect pollinators, and avian seed dispersers.

You are not only reaffirming the sanctity of life on this planet; you are actively participating in both ecological and social processes that allow it to thrive.

You are also asserting your membership in the *geo*political party that represents all species, races, cultures, genders, and faiths, caring *for* and communing *with* the many lives that matter to our collective survival.

Recently, I had a chance to amuse myself by performing the rather presumptuous if not preposterous act of planting something that will surely outlive me and perhaps not even flower until long after I am gone. I did so while working with a group of visitors on a little piece of land I tend on the outskirts of Patagonia, Arizona, not far from the US-Mexico border. These visitors had come to my hometown to spend a few days trying to understand what the term *border justice* means in one of the poorest, driest, and most historically degraded landscapes in the entire US.

To give my visitors an initial taste of the land itself, I invited them to eat with me and other locals and then to work with us for an hour or so on the task of transplanting several dozen agaves to hold the soil on the lips of some cobblestone terraces.

If you have not heard of them, agaves are long-lived, desert-adapted perennials with rosettes of succulent but leathery leaves. Some call them century plants, or mezcal. I had constructed those terraces a few years before in a rather vain attempt to capture rainfall and control soil loss on an eroding slope of red clay and gray limestone below my straw-bale home.

My guests had come from all over—Canada, Mexico, South Korea, and many parts of the US. They were individuals of all ages, colors, faiths, and cultures; some were of African, Asian, Middle Eastern, European, or Native American descent. I am sure that more than a few of them had never touched or seen an agave up close before. Its thorn-tipped, sword-shaped leaves have sharp spines running down their edges in a manner that still continues to intimidate me a half century after my first bloody initiation rite among them.

As I distributed these little thorny devils among my acquaintances, I suddenly realized that agaves are called century plants for a rather anthropocentric reason—most of us who transplant these succulents will never live long enough to see our own plantings flower, fruit, and die.

The plants themselves may not actually live for an entire century, but many of them will indeed outlive their propagators. Having turned sixty-five that very month, I conceded that it was unlikely that I would survive to see some of these agaves bloom or bear fruit.

I will have survived to be a very lucky elder if I am ever to taste their sweet, roasted flesh and fiber or to imbibe their fermented and distilled juices in a shot glass of mezcal.

And yet my visitors—many of whom would *never* return to this place over the rest of their lifetimes—were just as engaged as I was in this time-honored practice of agave propagation. It was a practice that had a two- to three-thousand-year-old legacy in this landscape, and we were simply playing a small role in collectively keeping that legacy alive.

One of my fellow propagators—an African American minister from North Carolina—later remarked to me that he was surprised how much he had been moved by the experience. There was something magical that came from getting down on his hands and knees and planting such a strange growth form into the parched earth. It refreshed his sense of hope and that of others around him. It was the kind of thing that his ancestors—and mine—had done since time immemorial, expressing our deep-seated human inclination to be curious and engaged with species much different from our own.

A month or so later, after taking my ninety-year-old mother to urgent care clinics and an emergency room to deal with a nagging problem with her heart, I came home exhausted, still a bit fearful that I might lose her that very week. And yet just before the sun went down, I decided to take some time out to transplant four more century plants that I had forgotten to put out for my visitors the month before.

That trivial act of caring for a species altogether dissimilar from my own occurred on a time scale different from that of the "urgent care" and "emergency" facilities I had just visited. It somehow *restored* my own determination to help my mother through her daunting crisis.

Just why do such measly gestures on behalf of other species continue to matter to us? In his 2017 book, *Two Paths: America Divided or United*, Republican statesman John Kasich recalled an epiphany he himself had during a time of crisis: "It came to me that most of us find satisfaction when we try to live a life bigger than ourselves . . . We need to look for ways to make a difference in the lives of others, in the world around us."

That may be why participating in biocultural restoration nearly always provides us with fresh insights and connections that are worth savoring. Working with people unlike ourselves tends to get us out of our bubble.

Still, why make a big deal about planting a couple of agaves? What's so special about working outdoors with someone else from another culture, race, profession, or faith?

It is true that over much of the course of human history, such endeavors were undoubtedly commonplace in many landscapes. But at *this* moment in time, these crosscutting gestures have become far too rare.

At the risk of belaboring a point that may already seem all too obvious to you, let me offer you a brief history of the discord that is putting many hard-won conservation advances of the last century at risk. I wish to do so for a very particular reason. I don't think we will see the urgency of embracing community-based restoration unless we are willing to concede that "mainstream" environmentalism has been under attack—if not "broken"—for some time.

What began as a nonpartisan effort to protect our planet has become one of the most perniciously divisive issues in public life. This division is not only undermining the robustness of our communities; it is also undermining the health of our landscapes, the survival of rare species, the diversity of our foodstuffs, and the food security of our communities. It's time we face up to the fact that we need a radical change in our modus operandi. And so let us consider the risks of living in a land divided.

CHAPTER 1

A Land Divided

Hᴀᴠᴇ ʏᴏᴜ ᴇᴠᴇʀ ꜰᴇʟᴛ ꜱᴏ ʀᴏᴏᴛᴇᴅ in a place that it was hard to remember where it began and your own body—or consciousness—ended? It is that feeling of oneness, of psychic safety, that pervades you when you feel in sync with your home, your landscape. Some of my Mexican American friends use the word *querencia* for such a feeling: that their deep affection and longing for the place where they grew up and the people who have nurtured it have come into some perfect alignment.

This is the feeling that this book hopes to instill: that by restoring the land and the connections with others in our community, we ourselves will feel healed and invigorated to do more tangible work on behalf of the many other lives around us.

It is also what my teacher, the Buddhist poet Gary Snyder, calls our "earth house hold" in his classic book by the same name. Sister Sharon Zayac, director of the Benincasa ecology and spirituality center in Springfield, Illinois, reminds us of the roots of that term: "*Eco* comes from the Greek word *oikos*, which means 'household.' It means 'home.' And home refers to the entire house—the whole planet Earth. *Ecology* means understanding all the relationships that make up the household. And humans are not the *only* denizens of the house . . . *Economy* refers to managing the household, a task at which, it is safe to say, we are miserably failing."

For a few moments, let us remind ourselves just *why* we are failing. To a large extent, it is because of the unbridled divisiveness we are experiencing in North America today compared to even a quarter century ago. And when I refer to "North America," I imagine our continent not as some homogeneous landscape seamlessly stretching "from sea to shining sea" but as a diverse patchwork of peoples of many colors living in wet and dry, steep and flat landscapes reaching from the Arctic Circle down to the Tropic of Cancer . . . or even farther south, to where Mesoamerica fully takes hold.

Yes, we've always had cultural differences, and those differences inevitably lead to social and political countercurrents as well as periodic conflicts. But that fact does not mean that we are fated to live on a battleground where stalemates keep our best intentions from being realized.

Today, you don't have to look very far for evidence that more and more Americans are "bowling alone," isolated from even their closest neighbors. Many of us now live in a bubble of sameness (surrounded by many other bubbles!) made possible by the silo-like nature of social media, cable television, ethnic enclaves, religious sects, and ideological cells.

Of particular concern to me is the palpable anger on either side of what James Gimpel has called "a gaping canyon-sized urban-rural chasm." This urban/rural divide has reshaped both state and national elections into "us vs. them" battles to determine who controls access to natural resources and social services.

For years, *Daily Yonder* founder Bill Bishop has warned about the clustering of like-minded citizens in ideologically isolated rural and urban areas. And now Bishop's prophetic warnings are being discussed, if not heeded, by many who formerly hid within their bubbles.

Why now? Well, it seems that the integrity of America is today so frayed that its citizens are *afraid* that it may fall into tatters. We have become the "house divided" that Abraham Lincoln warned us about, if our sharply divisive elections are any indicator.

In the national elections of 1976, only a quarter of US counties declared landslide victories for one party or the other, with the winners outdistancing their rivals by 20 percent or more of the vote. In the 2016 national elections, 80 percent of the counties in the US had landslide victories. In most of those counties, one dominant political party ran a full slate of like-minded souls, and they won every seat up for grabs.

You know how it goes: A Democrat might win most of the large, urban counties in the US but few of the 2,920 rural counties. If a Republican can win 2,500 of those smaller counties, he or she can dominate the electoral vote.

And if we know anything at all, it is that those different cohorts of voters looked through very different lenses at legislative actions like the Endangered Species Act, the Paris Climate Accord, offshore oil drilling, the Sage-Grouse Recovery Plan, the designation of national monuments, and the release of genetically engineered organisms.

One might justifiably argue that the two cohorts are not actually looking at the same thing at all.

Beneath headlines announcing the political victories of 2016 lay a disturbing subtext: the country's voters were split nearly fifty-fifty, with each party moving toward more extreme positions that were deeply distasteful to the other.

As Bill Bishop has concluded, "We have a geographically-fractured nation . . . We do seem to be splitting into two Americas where people can't comprehend the politics of the other side."

Of course, rural versus urban is not the only division plaguing our country. You yourself may be most concerned about one or more of America's other deep divides:

- the worsening relationship between African Americans and the "white" communities that often surround them;
- the fear of Native Americans that multinational mining companies and gas pipelines are running roughshod over their sovereign lands and sacred waters;
- the growing share of Hispanics who say that opportunities for *La Raza* are far more limited today than at any point in the new millennium;
- the unprecedented level of fear among Canadian and Mexican citizens as well as refugees from the Middle East and Africa about how the US policies will affect them;
- the increasing rates of hate crimes against Muslims, Jews, gays, lesbians, and transgender individuals; and
- the growing sense among blue-collar workers, elderly people, and college-age youth of being left behind economically as America's white-collar "one percent" gets tax cuts and bonuses.

By these and so many other indicators, Americans appear to be *at war* with one another rather than *at work* with one another. This trend has dire consequences for the health of both our communities and our landscapes.

More and more, the *jefes* and henchmen of gated communities, political lobbying groups, exclusive resorts, holier-than-thou churches and temples, wonky think tanks, and universities of privilege are not attempting to quell this unrest. Instead, they are feeding into and breeding deeper distrust of their neighbors. *Our neighbors.*

And that, my friends, brings us back to the profound shifts in American views of environmentalism that occurred in the wink of an eye after the first Earth Day in 1970.

As noted in Jedidiah Purdy's recent environmental retrospective, *After Nature*, 1970 was *the* year in US history when environmental issues had the very best chance of becoming the common ground on which all citizens gathered: "The new idea of ecology also promised a unifying challenge for a divided time. In his 1970 State of the Union address, President Nixon argued that environmental responsibility could unite Americans who were than split sharply over race and war. Picking up the cue, *Time* described the environmental crisis as an attractive 'problem which American skills . . . might actually solve, unlike the immensely more elusive problems of racial prejudice or the war in Viet Nam.'"

I experienced this hope personally when, while still a teenager, I served as a rather sleepy and disheveled Earth Day intern at the national headquarters in 1970. The summer following the first Earth Day event, I also worked as an unpaid environmental journalist and cartoonist for the nonprofit that was then known as Environmental Action.

Environmental Action was spearheaded by a young activist named Denis Hayes, whose charisma and visionary work has now enriched discussions in our society for four decades. Drawing on a motley crew of just a dozen of us in a small office on DuPont Circle, Denis set an inclusive tone and built a dynamic infrastructure for the first Earth Day.

This unprecedented planetary event magnanimously engaged more than twenty million Americans in celebrations, teach-ins, and sit-ins during April 1970. It became the largest environmental education event honoring mother earth in the history of humankind up until that time.

As a cub reporter for Environmental Action, I covered everything from the lead poisoning of children in Rust Belt factory towns to pesticide effects on birds and bees in midwestern farmlands. At that time, I sincerely believed that issues of environmental health would unite Americans, transcending lines of race and class. We would be galvanized by our desire to see both the government and industry get on with doing "the right thing."

Now, I personally wasn't exactly sure what that *right thing* would be. Nevertheless, I was assured by the more seasoned activists I worked for that grassroots political action on behalf of the environment and its many peoples could change America's moral trajectory.

Many of the staffers who mentored me were veterans of the civil rights summer in Selma and organizers of antiwar rallies held in Washington and across the nation. They believed that we, whether we lived in cities or rural towns, could come together to create healthier food and water, healthier families and communities, and healthier habitats for fish and wildlife. We seemed poised to make the environmental agenda a "shared space" in which people of all walks of life could participate.

Now fast-track ahead to nearly fifty years after that first Earth Day. To my surprise and remorse, between 1991 and 2016, Gallup Polls have tracked a 38 percent increase in the number of Americans who proudly (or cynically) proclaimed that they were *not* environmentalists.

As late as 1991, 37 percent of adult Americans surveyed claimed they were strong environmentalists, while another 41 percent conceded that the environmental label somewhat fit them.

But a quarter century later, only 23 percent of adult Americans claimed they were strong environmentalists, and another 19 percent reluctantly owned up to affiliating with one kind of environmental group or another.

A significant portion of the American public seemed to sense that something was terribly awry in both the government's natural resource agencies and the environmental movement as a whole. Those with misgivings had increased from just 19 percent in 1991 to 57 percent in 2016.

Think about it: that is an extraordinary shift in values over just twenty-five years. Has any similar change in public perceptions ever occurred that quickly? That shift has probably occurred in fits and starts, but it seemed set in concrete as the Great Recession leveled our economy in 2008. That's when many lower- and middle-class Americans began to wonder whether environmental regulations came at the expense of jobs and their own economic well-being.

Let me mince no words: individuals of *all classes and ethnicities* have felt increasingly disempowered by the prevalence of top-down decision-making about lands, wildlife, and plants that they had known and loved.

In many cases, they have become disenfranchised from policy-making processes that ignore their local knowledge, dismiss their cultural or faith-based values, and disregard impacts on their livelihoods.

By 2010, we had hit an all-time low point in this country's mood. Just 46 percent of Americans felt that the government was doing enough to protect the environment in ways that actually benefitted them. To most, government agencies' manners of regulation no longer make any sense.

Whenever I have visited rural communities over the last decade, I have noticed signs, placards, and bumper stickers that express a feeling that residents have "lost out." In coffee shops and taverns, I have overheard seething frustration that environmental decision-making was increasingly being done by some confederation of self-appointed experts that hardly seemed to care whether their communities were engaged.

I could feel a perplexing disconnect between people's love for their home ground and their disillusionment at having no ability to shape what would happen to it.

That very disconnect prompted a number of students of environmental conflict resolution to look at whether top-down "expertocracies" were having any more success in protecting environments than grassroots efforts. When E. Franklin Dukes and his colleagues compiled their findings in a landmark book called *Community-Based Collaboration*, Dukes himself came to four somewhat startling conclusions:

Programs and plans that are imposed upon resource-based
communities without authentic community participation in
crafting those plans *tend to fail miserably.*

Programs and plans involving natural resources that fail to
develop understanding and caring within affected human
communities *lend themselves to abuse.*

Programs and plans involving natural resource protection that
do not develop communal capacity to solve problems and
resolve conflicts *tend to fail.*

Programs and plans involving natural resource protection that
do not provide for ways of learning and adapting to change
tend to fail.

And yet failure, despair, and a sense of being disenfranchised do not
provide the entire picture. At the time I write this (in early 2018), Americans' level of concern about the environment and its relation to our food
security are approaching an all-time high.

Despite all the dire trends the pollsters have laid out, most Americans
still want to see conservation and restoration advance, but through a completely different paradigm, one rooted in true community engagement.

While many Americans express ever-deeper skepticism about the tac-
tics of government regulators and environmental experts, they still seem
to care deeply for "all of creation" and the richness of life on earth.

In 2017, 59 percent of Americans expressed alarm that the government was still not providing *enough* protection to threatened landscapes,
plants, and animals *in ways that they could sense* where they lived and
worked.

Didn't I hint a bit earlier that America might be suffering from some
bipolar disorder?

To capsulize a complex story in very few words, America is *not*
divided about whether the environment deserves restoration. They are

not divided about whether our communities require social healing. What divides us is *who* gets to decide *how* this work is done, *who* does it, and *how much* it should cost. If we can come to terms with these questions, by means other than more regulation, all the more people will be fully onboard with conservation and restoration.

And that, methinks, is how community-based collaboration in bio-cultural restoration can bring people of diverse viewpoints together in a place we now call the radical center.

It is how we can bridge that (virtual) Grand Canyon–sized chasm in our society that some call the great divide.

It is where we can start healing the wounds in ourselves, in our communities, and in the land.

I am not alone in believing that this approach can move us in the right direction. I can hear it in the words of Melissa Nelson of the Cultural Conservancy in California; of Will Allen of Growing Power in Wisconsin; of Winona LaDuke of the Anishinaabeg on the White Earth reservation in Minnesota; of Miguel Santestevan at Sol Feliz Farm in New Mexico; of Peter Forbes, founding director of the Center for Whole Communities in Vermont; of Veronica Kyle of Faith in Place in Illinois; and of Courtney White, who founded the Quivira Coalition in New Mexico.

In a seminal essay called "The Promise of Community-Based Collaboration," E. Franklin Dukes seems to share in my optimism: "There is an absolute need for such work. If we are to have communities sustained ecologically, socially and economically, it is essential that a capacity for productive, collaborative, place-based decision processes be developed."

And so, in this humble little book, I will argue that one of the best ways to heal the divisions that have been plaguing us is for people to work hand in hand to heal the land. By doing so, we can reduce the depth of the divides in our communities, not just the gullies in our landscapes. And when we have done so, we can then celebrate our work around a shared table with the fruits of our labors.

But in order to accomplish such work wisely, we need to understand the importance of collaboration. Without it, we are left with the top-down approaches still used by some natural resources managers—approaches that leave communities feeling dispossessed and disempowered. Collaboration, as an alternative mode of action and decision-making, moves us away from the shout-downs that have given both monkeywrenching environmental activism and the Tea Party resistance to it their bad names.

Changing this dynamic is key to a kind of community-based restoration that benefits us all (and other species as well). How to create that change is the focus of the very next part of this story.

CHAPTER 2

Farming in the Radical Center

Have you ever savored the ripe fruits or fresh vegetables from land that you yourself had begun to restore perhaps just a few years before? If not, does land restoration seem like an abstract concept with which you have no hands-on experience? Do habitat restoration and species recovery feel like things that happen off in the distance, beyond your sight, your earshot, your taste buds, and your nostrils?

Ironically, the fruits of restoration are already all around you, though they may not be explicitly presented to you in that manner.

In North America today, you can partake of some 628 species of cultivated food plants and 14 species of livestock, in addition to at least 4,000 types of wild plants and species of fish and game. Your increased access to this diversity of foods is largely due to the collaborative conservation and restoration efforts of a variety of farmers, fishers, foresters, foragers, ranchers, chefs, orchard keepers, and discerning eaters on this continent.

Over the course of the following stories, I'll be encouraging you to savor some of that great diversity of foods, but I'll also be inviting you to *taste and see* the world from which those foods spring in an entirely different manner: Tasting the huckleberries with a sense of when fire last moved through that patch of berry bushes . . . Digging for camas after seeing their wet prairie habitat freed from the competition of invasive species . . . Hooking a Chinook salmon and smoking it over alder wood after learning how stream restoration allowed it to migrate up into the headwaters from the sea . . . Grilling a bison burger after helping bring down the fences to let the buffalo roam, creating wallows that other creatures and plants use along the way . . .

Such place-based foods may begin to bless your table more frequently than they did in the past, but the fruits of restoration do not appear all at once, nor are all of them edible. Some of the rewards, in fact, are social, for the roots of the trees we plant with neighbors begin to bind us together. Most importantly, these efforts can break down our stereotypes, as a woman from a salmon restoration project once brought home to me.

I encountered her in a workshop of the Society for Ecological Restoration, and although I no longer remember her name, I will never forget how humbled I felt by her message. This middle-aged woman came into our workshop to offer a twenty-minute talk after half of the session was over. She sat down in a crowded room among a couple dozen young environmentalists excited by the fact that President Clinton and Forest Service director Jack Ward Thomas had just put twenty-four million acres of old growth forests in their region under ecosystem management. It was not long after the federal listing of northern spotted owls had forced the closure of industrial-scale logging in many national forests, and thousands of loggers had lost their jobs. The youth in the room were not only jazzed that "their side" had won a major environmental victory. They were also hopeful that now forest restoration would be funded on an unprecedented scale—the equivalent land area of four Connecticuts.

As this latecomer stood up to be introduced and offer the next talk, the mood in the room shifted. I perked up. Perhaps it was because the next speaker looked so different from many others at the conference.

While the vast majority of participants wore Teva sandals, khaki shorts, green fleeces, and brightly colored T-shirts with outrageous drawings and in-your-face slogans in defense of mother earth, she wore a pastel, Western-style pantsuit, a silk blouse, and boots. As she spoke her very first word to us, I could sense male attendees dismissing her because of her dress, her beauty-parlor hairdo, and her vaguely rural Western accent.

She started off by explaining that she was there because her husband had been one of the loggers who had lost his job when the FEMAT logging closures began to go into effect. Just hearing that she was from a family of loggers made the group uncomfortable. Their collective body language grew irritated, even hostile. Even when she began to describe how she and her husband had recruited jobless loggers to join them in restoring salmon streams, most of the men in the room were tapping their pencils, looking out the windows, or staring at their laptop screens.

But then this "stranger in a strange land" did the most flabbergasting thing, *right in the middle of the twenty minutes allotted to her.* She asked if we could take a two-minute break so that she could use the women's room and suggested that because she could still finish her talk in the allotted time, we should all stay put. When she abruptly left the room, there were curses, barbs, and wisecracks that do not bear repeating. And yet everyone stayed in the room as they had been politely asked to do.

When the woman returned, she was dressed in a fleece, T-shirt, khaki shorts, and Tevas; her hair was pulled back into a ponytail. She moved out *in front* of the podium, and to the best of my recollection, said something like this:

"Listen up. A few minutes ago, you dismissed me on the basis of my dress and my accent. But I'll tell you what: I will not let you dismiss the work that the fine men that my husband and I have recruited are doing in this region. They are healing the very streams and wildlife habitats that some of you in this room have worked to protect! You need their work as much as they need yours. But to join forces on behalf of the fish and wildlife we all want to see survive, you have to first acknowledge the value of the men and women who care about the same things you do but who don't talk about them with the same words you do."

To say that I was appalled and embarrassed by my own prejudices is an understatement. My colleagues and I had hardly offered this courageous, compassionate, and intelligent woman the time of day, let alone any deeper listening. She simply did not look like a member of our "club" of conservationists. That was the day I decided that I needed to quit the club I had been in—consciously or unconsciously—for most of my life. To this day, I remain grateful to this performance artist who had found a novel way to speak truth to power—in this case, the power of the expertocracy.

In memory of that moment, I encourage *all of us* to imagine something other than the infamous zero-sum game *that is stalemating our country*. We need to interact with each other differently, taking a more inclusive approach to decision-making and restoration.

In *Stitching the West Back Together*, my old friends Tom Sheridan, Nathan Sayre, and David Seibert explain why it's time we engage rather than alienate the diverse voices in our rural and urban communities. They want us to regard everyone—farmworkers and loggers, cafeteria cooks and wild foragers, hunters and fly-fishers, teachers and preachers, ranchers and career professionals in agencies—as equal partners in collective efforts to "stitch back together" our damaged landscapes and communities.

Each time such diverse players come together, we should get in the habit of asking six fundamental questions:

1. Do you sense that this restorative work might address the deepest practical needs that you, your family, and your neighbors must fill to continue living with dignity in your community?

2. Might it build toward some moral common ground that will allow your community members to be better lasting stewards of the resources in your home place?

3. Does it strengthen your community's overall capacity to collectively solve problems, reduce disparities, and resolve conflicts with novel solutions?

4. Will working together through more equitable processes foster you and your neighbors' own well-being, intellectual growth, neighborliness, and organizational capacity?

5. Will it help all of you to better safeguard what makes your place unique and offer you more lasting solutions in the face of uncertainty?

6. Will being engaged in this collaboration be pleasurable for you, allowing you to taste, see, smell, and hear the fruits of your collective labors? *Or will it simply be another tedious obligation to attend seemingly endless meetings and hearings where no one really listens to anyone else?*

If you choose to ask such questions, they may help you move toward some immediate reduction in conflicts. But you cannot count on pat answers or flash-in-the-pan solutions to carry you very far. Be cautious of instant claims of success, like *We planted three hundred trees today and now the forest (or orchard) looks like it is restored!*

A sequoia forest cannot be restored in a single a day, nor can a diverse pollinator guild be reassembled merely by sowing nectar-rich plants on a single farm. It takes efforts across administrative and property boundaries so that changes ripple out through an entire foodshed and patient capital can be invested over decades.

In the end, the benefits of restoration will be far more than what you grow on your farm, what you harvest from a nearby forest patch, or what ends up on your plate. Being part of collaborative restoration involves the slow-growing fruits and steady dividends of long-term social engagement. It is ultimately about *place-making* and *peace-making*—in your community's meeting rooms and council halls, on farms and ranches, around forests and lakes, and at many tables. Its goal is that all may reap the many tangible and intangible benefits of community-based collaborations.

In the past, many of us who wanted to restore landscapes or help species recover were obsessed with outcomes; in other words, we were emphatically *content*-driven. We only began to pay sufficient attention to social *process* when our neglect of it began to trip us up and undermine our goals. Count me among the ranks of those content-driven geeks who must have seemed narrowly focused and marginally collaborative to members of the first few communities I worked within.

In fact, I initially missed the significance of a landmark event that occurred near my desert home in October 1999, when the Community-Based Collaborative Research Consortium was founded. Forty funders, facilitators, researchers, activists, and community members met in Tucson, Arizona, just a few miles from where I was working at the time. Did I even catch wind of their proximity?

How could I have neglected such an extraordinary convergence happening on my home ground? Well, it is probably because I was (and still am) a recovering "content geek." As a matter of fact, if I had tried to write this story for you even a half dozen years ago, I would have led it off in a completely different manner that I am attempting today.

Perhaps I would have tried to baffle you with scholarly bullshit . . . or numb you with impressive numbers . . . or entangle you with technical assertions to convince you of how bright *and* right I was about how to conserve land, recover species, and farm sustainably.

But after suffering from a rash of concussions and various other personal setbacks a few years ago, I no longer "feel" that I was ever that bright or particularly right about anything at all . . . at least not when I compare my insights to those of the many good people around me.

Instead, I feel grateful to still be alive during this precious moment on earth, when I can rub shoulders, fins, and wings with lives quite different from my own.

I am stunned and humbled by the capacity for innovation found in every heterogeneous community where I have had the chance to work. I no longer assume that I personally have some unique ability to provide answers to the nagging problems plaguing my community, our society at large, or the food-producing landscapes we depend on.

It's not that I have lost complete confidence in all my old environmental values, skills, and convictions. It's more that I have gained deep respect for the validity of values, skills, and convictions quite different from the ones I grew up with. And in this case, by "growing up," I mean the maturation process that those of us who were involved in the environmental movement have undergone since that first Earth Day in 1970.

As I hinted at in the last chapter, that Earth Day was somewhat of a benchmark for me and for many other baby boomers. In my case, it was not merely because I turned eighteen the year of the first global Earth Day celebration. It had more to do with my taking a first look into a world that was far more diverse—but also much more imperiled—than any I had experienced as an infant, adolescent, or young adult.

Through working for Earth Day, I came of age as the environmental movement itself came of age. And it was my rite of passage. It was also a benchmark year in the minds of many other Americans as we witnessed a meteoric rise in the public discussion of environmental books, films, and exhibits as well as an increase in the number of federal agencies and laws aimed at protecting the environment from further harm.

By happenstance, really, I was lucky enough to be blessed with provocative but all-too-brief personal encounters with environmentalists like

Ralph Nader, Barry Commoner, Dorothy "Save the Dunes" Buell, Gaylord Nelson, Pete Seeger, Stewart Udall, Ed Abbey, and Gary Snyder—even before I reached the age of twenty-one. Such close encounters with the big dogs of environmentalism no doubt heightened my fervor to save the earth.

And yet, over the last half century, people of many different faiths, races, livelihoods, disciplines, and persuasions have sometimes gradually—and at other times dramatically and radically—changed my views. They have made me question my assumptions about the values that historically drove environmental work . . . and much of what we have more recently failed to achieve.

I am not alone. The collaborative conservation movement is being built by individuals who see inclusivity as both a social and environmental imperative.

In appendix 1 of this book, I've laid out some of the paradigm shifts that have begun to occur since the earliest days of the environmental movement. In "conservation couplets," I juxtapose conventional protectionist approaches with the community-centered sensibilities that are taking root all around us.

For the moment, I simply want to offer you just one of the couplets:

We were once told that "the one process now going on that will take millions of years to correct is loss of genetic and species diversity by the destruction of natural habitats. This is the folly for which our descendants are least likely to forgive us."

We can now see that when we put aside our differences, "we have the collective capacity to recover varieties, species, communities, and habitat types that had been on the brink of extinction, and to witness, taste, and celebrate their flourishing once again."

The first statement tries to motivate us through guilt, implying that we have destroyed biodiversity through either ignorance or greed. Intentionally or not, it suggests that we have perpetrated an unforgivable act so that not only the blame but also the burden of restitution falls squarely on our shoulders.

The counterpoint statement does not rely on accusations. It does acknowledge that there have been both historic and recent reductions in diversity, but it reminds us that there is still much that has not yet been lost that we can caringly attend to. And it puts forward a goal that offers all of us tangible rewards: *to witness, taste, and celebrate their flourishing once again.*

However enticing the latter vision might seem, there's a hurdle that keeps many of us from fully participating in this paradigm shift: we're hanging on to extreme, judgmental views of others whose ideas, and voting records, don't exactly match up with our own.

We must be willing to take a step toward consensus, even when it means risking criticisms from mudslingers on the far extremes. This fertile middle ground is what rancher Bill McDonald began to refer to in the mid-1990s as "the Radical Center."

It's the very phrase that my friend Courtney White used to kick-start a collaborative conservation movement in the West. It was less than four years after the landmark Community-Based Collaboration event in Tucson when he brought Bill and two dozen more of us together for three days in 2003. That meeting gave us a chance to drill down on the promise of resolving conflicts on food-producing lands in the American West.

It began in a rather modest manner. Twenty-some participants simply hung out and listened deeply to one another in a hotel room in Albuquerque. Gradually, we shared and then put aside most of our minor differences, realizing that all of us had dedicated our entire lives to similar big-picture goals. We began to improvise, to cajole and caress into existence a manifesto that Courtney eventually called "An Invitation to Join the Radical Center."

But that invitation was only the beginning of our consensus-building efforts. The Radical Center Manifesto is now a living document signed and supported by tens of thousands of individuals and hundreds of community organizations all around North America. And to my delight, I've recently learned that farmers and their food distributors have been working on a similar set of "common ground" principles that they call the Middle Path.

Of course, there are skeptics who adamantly maintain that the radical center is just a euphemism for sitting on the fence or trying to please everyone and satisfying no one. They claim such ambivalence can do more harm than good. Or they fear that community-based conservation relinquishes too much decision-making power to the local level, disparaging federal and international conservation efforts.

But in her thoughtful and humor-filled book about resolving rangeland conflicts, *A Place for Dialogue*, Sharon MacKenzie Stevens turns the fence-sitting criticism on its head: "What I have had to learn is that sitting on a fence need not lead to distance or helplessness. Instead, by granting validity to multiple beliefs and inventions, symmetrical analysis demonstrates that possibilities are not as limited as they might at first seem. [Entertaining perspectives on the environment different from your own] simply highlights the role of human agency in creating and choosing among different possible socioecological futures. Fence-sitting, therefore can create new openings for agency, rather than foreclosing grounds for decision-making."

In short, a stance (or dance!) in the radical center is not some wishy-washy compromise by those who are unable to choose a side on which to stand. It is not *ambivalent*; its strength is that it is *multivalent*. It is a disciplined position of listening intently and taking into account voices other than your own.

That's when creative tension ferments, allowing solutions to bubble up from a brew of diverse perspectives—prismatic solutions that no single view could offer on its own.

As one of my Quaker friends once asked me, "How can they hope to engage others in the restoration of biodiversity if they are reluctant to let the awesome complexity of human diversity into the decision-making room?"

This idea—that diversity creates rather than blocks solutions—has simultaneously emerged in many independent community discussions.

To be sure, the elaboration of "the radical center" did not begin—nor will it end—with Bill McDonald and Courtney White, just as Aldo Leopold did not independently devise *the* land ethic for all peoples for all time. They simply put a tag line on a social process that has been articulated and practiced by exemplary individuals and communities for centuries. It has often emerged out of deadlock, when people begin to realize that piecemeal solutions quickly become devastatingly obsolete.

Recently, William McDowell, who was trained in the same University of Arizona natural resources programs I went through, recounted to me what he's learned over his years working in agricultural communities with the Clark Fork Coalition in Montana: "To this day, I've never figured out anything that works better in rural communities than one-on-one relationship building. I've always been able to talk to anybody, but I've really had to learn *to listen* to their needs instead of just pitching to them my own organization's ideas. I'll never forget the Montana stockman who came up to shake my hand and say to me, *'If you care that I stay in business as a rancher, fine, let's exchange some ideas. If not, I'm done talking to you right now.'*"

After repeated failures to win someone over to their agenda, environmentalists are often compelled to seek new ways to reframe their concerns—in ways more compatible with that person's values. This begins a dance at the radical center that is actually much older than the collaborative restoration movement itself.

In fact, an intentional stance in the radical center may date back at least one thousand years to the time of St. Francis of Assisi—the so-called patron saint of ecology and restorative justice. St. Francis found common ground among Muslims and Christian believers, among the poor and the rich, among the laity and the cloistered, among farmers and wolves.

This third way emerged in other enclaves of so-called Western (Judeo-Christian-Muslim) culture as well. It may well be far older and much more widespread in Eastern and indigenous cultures. And yet it has been practiced by the likes of Buddha and Gandhi, Abraham Lincoln and Jane Addams, Nelson Mandela and John Mohawk, Dolores Huerta and Martin Luther King Jr., John Kasich and Richard Rohr.

I presume that most if not all of you already respect the dignity of those unlike yourselves in race, class, faith, party preference, or world view. But what I am arguing for is your personal engagement in restorative processes that might add an additional dimension to your respect for diversity.

By delving into the "dirty" (read "earthly") work of restoration, we are joining together, not merely with other human beings, but with other life-forms as well. By doing so, we begin to tell a different story than the one we typically hear on the news.

We are *restorying* our collective cultural memory, not just *restoring* the land, its waters, plant life, animal life, and microbial lives. We are acting out a fresh way of behaving that is, in and of itself, an antidote to despair and an antibody against acrimony.

We step back into some ancient ritualized dance of shared destiny, one that the nature poet Robert Bly refers to as "sleepers joining hands." In short, we return to do together what is richest for our species as a whole, something that can only come through rediversifying and enriching the landscapes in which we live.

As with most things, action to restore our continent's food-producing capacity speaks louder than words. So let's see what collaborative conservation looks like on the ground.

CHAPTER 3

Will Work for Dirt

Have you ever tried to grow a garden in your backyard, only to find that the dirt was too worn-out and dry to produce anything? Have you coaxed that soil back to life so that it, in turn, could give life to fruits, vegetables, or root crops?

Gabriela Valeria Villavicencio Valdez, an urban garden enthusiast in Querétaro, Mexico, is all too familiar with lifeless dirt. In fact, she has adopted a newly coined name for this type of postapocalyptic, dystopian, metro soil: *urbic technosol transportic.*

Gabriela pointed some out to me in a vacant lot where a building was recently demolished. The site was littered with asphalt, pieces of chalky wallboard, metal, fired clay bricks, and concrete. And yet tenacious families were trying to cultivate this "soil" to grow vegetables in a barrio in the burgeoning city of Querétaro. That's where close to a million people try to eke out a living on the southern edges of the Chihuahuan Desert.

If have you ever tried to garden in such a place—where dark, rich topsoil seems as rare as gold—just remember that you are not alone.

In 1950, just 64.7 percent of Americans lived in cities, but by 2015, that percentage had surpassed 80 percent. By 2030, it will likely approach

87 percent. We have become an urban species, living in places where it is increasingly hard to grow food.

Unfortunately, it is not just cities where soil is in bad shape. In areas urban and rural, land is becoming dirt-poor, lacking the humus, moisture, and microbes needed to grow healthy food. In fact, a third of the world's land surface—especially under gardens, orchards, fields, irrigated pastures, and rangelands—is no longer as productive as it once was.

Soil scientists who gathered in 2015 to advise the UN Food and Agricultural Organization were astonished at just how quickly microbes are disappearing from the world's soils and how quickly foods grown in those soils are losing their nutritive value. They were equally horrified that this loss is directly impoverishing peoples who are already among the hungriest and most profoundly marginalized in our society.

All told, the capacity to feed ourselves has been declining by one-half percent per year. If these trends continue, our descendants will have nothing to share for dinner other than "stone soup" and "rock-ette salad."

And yet there is much that can be—and is being—done to prevent that from happening. There is good evidence that soil fertility and microbial diversity can be restored for healthy food production in less than a decade—even in metro areas where *urbic technosols* currently prevail.

In fact, a grassroots effort aimed at slowing erosion *and* restoring America's soils has been swelling for decades. In many ways, it remains one of the best examples of community-based collaboration ever seen on the North American continent. This work has widened to restore wild habitats such as trout streams, grasslands where bison roam and prairie chickens peck, and scrublands for sage-grouse. It has been performed by loose confederations of local landowners who democratically decide how to manage farmlands, ranchlands, community gardens, and green belt forests on the outskirts of urban areas.

Collectively, these local nodes form a network known as the National Association of Conservation Districts (NACD). Today, there are some three thousand districts engaging more than seventeen thousand volunteers.

A turning point in dealing with soil erosion occurred in 1981, when Neil Sampson, executive vice president of NACD, sounded an alarm that was heard across the entire continent. In *Farmland or Wasteland: A Time to Choose*, Sampson warned that Iowa corn farmers were losing as much as fifteen tons of topsoil per acre each year, and wheat farmers were losing as much as twenty tons per acre.

About the time Sampson was writing, a report in the *British Food Journal* found that from 1930 to 1980, the nutrient content in twenty vegetables had fallen, most likely as soils were depleted; the average calcium content had declined 19 percent; iron declined 22 percent; and potassium declined 14 percent. Several more recent studies corroborate this phenomenon, linking nutritional value to soil health. According to Dakota stockman Gabe Brown, we would need to eat four to eight times the volume of certain fruits and vegetables to obtain the same nutrient levels from our food crops that people enjoyed in the early twentieth century!

As such devastating research began to appear in scientific journals, Sampson and others pushed hard to see that the Soil and Water Conservation Act was fully implemented in 1977. By then more than a tenth of American farmland was eroding at annual rates of more than fourteen tons of soil per acre. In 1982, farmers were still losing 1.68 billion tons of soil per year from water erosion and 1.38 billion tons per year from wind erosion.

Sampson was both eloquent and blunt enough to tell farmers that if such losses went on any longer, their livelihoods would be going to hell in a hand basket. That is when farmers and ranchers decided that a loss of even seven tons per acre was unacceptable. They simply would not survive as food producers.

Gradually, with perseverance and shared know-how, tens of thousands of farmers in the three thousand conservation districts began to put more stringent erosion control measures in place. By 2007, they had cut levels of stormwater-caused "sheet and rill" erosion almost in half and losses from wind erosion by a third.

In less than a quarter century, they had found cost-effective means of reducing the total rate of erosion on the average acre of farmland from 7.3 tons to 4.8 tons, a 43 percent decrease! They were conserving 1.33 billion tons more topsoil than they had been in 1981, when Sampson had let loose his warning cry.

Although various conservation districts around the country did not congeal into a national association until 1946, the origin of this grassroots approach to farmland restoration can be traced back at least as far as 1934. That's when Hugh Bennett, head of the fledgling US Soil Erosion Service, asked forester and wildlife ecologist Aldo Leopold to drive with him out to Coon Valley, Wisconsin. They wanted to see what could be done to restore a highly eroded, economically devastated watershed in the area.

What these two nationally renowned experts did when they got out to Coon Valley is the perhaps most astonishing moment in their entire decade-long adventure together. They went into a small café where many of the farmers came for a cup of coffee and breakfast, and they simply *listened*.

They *listened* to what the farmers themselves said had happened to their watershed. They *listened* to how they felt affected by the problems this degradation had caused. And they *listened* to what the farmers thought they could do about it if given some technical support and added manpower.

After coffee, the farmers and stockmen took Leopold and Bennett out into the mudslides and gullies to figure out how they could be mended. And when the breakfast café became a bar serving drinks in the late afternoon, they took Bennett and Leopold back there to develop a plan for getting the work done. Leopold and Bennett listened again, abdicating their roles as top-down experts. Together with the farmers, they created a demonstration project for what they soon began to call "cooperative conservation," what we call community-based collaborative restoration today.

As Bennett and Leopold came back to that Coon Valley café week after week, they brought with them workers from the Civilian Conservation Corps (CCC), student interns from the University of Wisconsin, soil scientists, and foresters from the USDA and from state agencies. Pretty soon, they were on the ground together, restoring soils, healing downcut watercourses, filling in gullies, reseeding hillsides, modifying crop rotations and grazing practices, planting trees in windbreaks to stabilize stream banks, and shaping contour terraces in fields and pastures above the streams.

Some 418 farming families and two hundred additional workers from the CCC and university's internship programs eventually participated in the restoration of more than forty thousand acres of food-producing lands in Coon Valley. As Leopold later noted, they had come together to "show that integrated use is possible on private farms, and that such integration is mutually advantageous to both the landowners and the public."

One direct benefit of this collaborative effort did not fully emerge until a half century after the demonstration project. The farmers' descendants decided to form a vegetable and dairy cooperative that they called CROPP—the Coulee Region Organic Produce Pool. CROPP is well-known to many of us today through its brand of foods, Organic Valley. Its headquarters is located in LaFarge, Wisconsin, just twenty-five miles away from the heart of Coon Valley.

Today, the cooperative has expanded to include more than two thousand farmer-owners in at least thirty-three states and four Canadian provinces.

And yet it can be argued that all of CROPP's members and consumers now reap the benefits of a participatory process that began in Coon Valley. If anyone doubts that farmland restoration can pay for itself, simply cite Organic Valley's $1.1 billion of food sales in 2016.

I once met one of CROPP's founders almost by accident, and the elderly dairyman treated me to a story about building Organic Valley from the ground up:

"When I first told my wife, my brothers, and brothers-in-law that I was going to put some of our life savings into help starting a food marketing cooperative, they looked at me like I was nuts. You know, rural residents tend to be somewhat risk-aversive as well as economically and politically conservative sometimes . . . In fact, one of my family members initially asked me, 'What's a Collective? Isn't that some kind of communist plot to infiltrate our farming communities?'"

"Anyway, by the time all my royalty and revenue checks from CROPP over the years had amounted to a million dollars of returns, they all wanted to become that brand of communist!"

The collaborations that Bennett and Leopold facilitated have made an important contribution to soil health. But much more needs to be done to hold soil in place and to bring life back into the soil and onto the land.

We can join with friends and neighbors to gather up postharvest crop debris, spoiled produce, and livestock manure to make compost, not dust bowls.

We can build brush weirs and living fencerows wherever wounded floodplain land needs a little help from its friends.

But it's not just about keeping bad erosion from happening; it's also about restoring "the good" to the soil in terms of its fertility and tilth, its beneficial invertebrate diversity, and its microbial richness.

Most importantly, we can form social networks to restore the soil—actually imitating the mycorrhizal fungal networks in healthy soils. By collectively practicing such biomimicry, we can provide soils across

entire watersheds a chance to accumulate moisture, nutrients, and a myr-
iad of beneficial microbes that may be out of sight but not out of work.

I personally find this work much more satisfying when I perform it
with others. I prefer to be a member of a work crew that is out to prove
the axiom *"Many hands make for light work."*

I recently reflected on this axiom of "social thermodynamics" while
working with a group of teenagers in a summer program called Borderlands Earth Care Youth. We were on a steep slope of my rocky ridge,
building terraces to stop erosion. The goal was to support the roots of
edible desert plants like mesquite, prickly-pear cactus, and agaves.

I had cofounded the program five years before. Now I stood there
amazed by both the raw energy and deep willingness of a dozen young
men and women to get their hands dirty and their T-shirts sweaty on a
day when temperatures soared over 105 degrees.

The dozen high school students from my hometown of Patagonia are
among the nearly one hundred Earth Care Youth who have participated
in the first six years of our program, which has now spread to the nearby
towns of Douglas-Agua Prieta and Ambos Nogales. They had arrived
before seven that morning and were moving cobbles and boulders into
place within minutes of hitting the ground.

I had begun the terracing five years before, keylining the slope with
my young friend Caleb Weaver, who had since become the coordinator
of Borderlands Earth Care Youth. At that time, the slope was near barren
except for a few drought-stressed mesquite saplings; it held a scatter of
withered clumps of grass, but whenever it rained, most of the slope lost
more soil than it gained.

Caleb and I had put the first few terraces or *trincheras* in place that
summer but didn't quite realize that they would need so much annual
maintenance. We now conceded that cobblestones love gravity so much
that they seem to slink downhill of their own volition, leaving the
trincheras looking like a series of dotted lines.

After a bad fall on a similar slope in the Big Bend of Texas that precipitated two knee surgeries, I lost a year and a half of maintenance time on that slope at home. It was a sorry sight when the Borderlands Earth Care Youth crew arrived, but within two hours, they had worked it back into a beautiful symmetry of curvilinear terraces running across the slope.

Not only that, but the mesquite trees were pruned into umbrella-like canopies, and among them, the young people transplanted more hardy perennials, just as my guests from North Carolina had done a few months before.

And much to my surprise, where the dots in the dotted line had held fast over the last four years, rich, moist soil was accumulating. Plants were getting taller, branching, and flowering. A harvest of edibles was just around the corner, and they could not have gotten this far without the kindness of strangers.

I was grateful for the goodwill of the Borderlands Earth Care Youth, but I was also grateful for the kindness of the "microbial strangers" who were hidden from sight in the little mounds of topsoil that were accumulating behind each terrace.

While the Earth Care volunteers had names like Ben, Eden, Carlitos, Alysia, Felix, and Johnnie, this other set of allies went by stranger names. They are known as arbuscular mycorrhiza in the fungal phylum, which scientists refer to as the Glomeromycota, and include several hundred species, such as our local jack-of-all-trades, *Glomus deserticola*. These soil fungi are allies to plants. They communicate across underground networks through chemical signals, guiding both nutrient uptake and defense mechanisms in the trees connected by them.

Forest ecologist Suzanne Simard playfully calls such networks—the largest covering more than 2,500 acres of forest in the Pacific Northwest—the "wood wide web." We are not the only species to send life-affirming communiqués across long distances!

Whatever we call these systems of mutual support, we must return microbes to the soil if we want healthy habitats. Without them, we will lose the forest for the sake of a few disconnected trees.

Of course, there are two ways to restore beneficial soil microbes to a landscape. The first is to apply a liquefied mixture of microbes as an inoculant, assuming that its organisms are appropriate for the environment.

But you can also do it the old-fashioned way. The second method is to encourage the microbes to voluntarily set up shop in your neighborhood. By building structures that control erosion, you guide the microbes, along with sediment and detritus, to flow with rainwater and settle in the places you are attempting to heal.

The question of how to slow erosion was on my mind forty years ago, when I spent a winter with traditional farmers in semiarid watersheds on the flanks of the Sierra Madre Occidental. Recently, I returned to roughly the same landscape in Sonora, Mexico. This time, I had a different set of questions rolling around in my head:

How might these farmers maintain the microbial diversity of their soils without "formally inoculating" them?

Why and how do they choose to work with neighbors whose livelihoods are different from their own?

Why are they willing to invest their own time and money to restore "ecosystem services" when farmers and ranchers in other regions of Mexico won't do so unless they get paid by the government?

The short answer to these questions is that they had gained confidence in the return on the investments their community made by collectively maintaining living fencerows. If just one of them had put fencerows on his property, few benefits would have accrued. Of course, more complete answers required some investigation, so I invited fifteen of my oldest friends and finest students—cultural geographers, photographers, range managers, plant ecologists, hydrologists, ecosystem scientists, and watershed management workers—to join me in Sonora.

There we spent a week documenting an informal but deeply rooted practice that has persisted among Sonoran farmers, ranchers, and orchard keepers for upwards of three hundred years: the building of living fencerows. We awakened at four thirty in the morning and went out into the agrarian landscapes of Sonora to work until the summer temperatures reached over a hundred degrees Fahrenheit before noon. Then we went back into the closest village and compiled our interviews, plant samples, bird tallies, crop descriptions, and measurements of soil volumes.

The fencerows in Sonora are deceptively simple in both composition and design. Most comprise seven- to nine-foot cottonwood and willow branches that are pruned from older trees. They are then placed as live stakes in the sandy streambeds that run along the banks of the floodplain that edge arable fields, pastures, and orchards.

The fencerows can be straight as an arrow for a hundred yards or so, or they can become curvilinear, following the intermittent stream as it meanders through the desert. Most of the fencerows include not only the live willow and cottonwood stakes that bloom and root in early spring—becoming rapidly growing saplings—but also leafy branches that are woven in between the trunks of these saplings.

These woven fences or brush weirs break the force of the seasonal floods that come on the heels of summer monsoons. And as I was soon to learn, by encouraging detritus to settle in the fields after the rains, the fences were recruiting an active mycorrhizal community. In each handful of this silty, flood-washed debris, I could see the lacework of fuzzy fungal hyphae, rich in nutrients and carbon.

Unlike the hard riprap used to stabilize streambanks elsewhere, porous brush weirs allow the floods to slowly flow onto the fields, enriching them with a fresh layer of organics. It is much like the strategies used by ancient Egyptian farmers who relied on inundations along the floodplain of the River Nile to annually renew the fertility of their fields.

But that is not all, the farmers explained to us. On the Rio Sonora floodplain below the pueblo of Chinapa, two brothers—Armando and Gilberto Madero—showed us two parallel fencerows of willow saplings that had been planted nine years apart.

The first was planted immediately after a major flood scoured out the fields' barbed-wire fence and a twenty-foot swath of soil that had been left unprotected. They planted the second a few years later on the edge of the soil bank that had been freshly deposited by less damaging floods. Once the Maderos planted the two bank-stabilizing fencerows, the next few floods did little damage.

In fact, during the nine-year period in which both fencerows were functioning, Gilberto and Armando captured more than 325 cubic yards of nutrient-rich topsoil. The fencerows had slowed down the *agua puerca* ("dirt-rich waters") so that it deposited its *abono del rio* ("river-churned compost or green manure") right where it was needed most.

The brothers then planted crops such as chili peppers, maize, and beans in their now-fertile fields. The very same floods that devastated nearby fields had blessed the Maderos with such an influx of organic matter that they did not have to fertilize their maize for another seven years!

I do not want to single out the Madero brothers as if they are the only conservationists in their community, working like small islands in a sea of industrial farmers. The majority of their neighbors—rich or poor, elderly or youthful—exerted as much effort in maintaining their fencerows as the Maderos did.

A few, however, were doing their piece of the collective work in isolation: a single farmer planting a stand-alone fencerow. In contrast, the Maderos were part of a group of farmers who helped one another plant, prune, and manage several contiguous miles of well-tended fencerows. They also informally collaborated with neighboring orchard keepers, ranchers, mezcal distillers, municipal well managers, and road maintenance workers to keep the fencerows intact.

This informal group was connected through family ties, small business partnerships, high school friendships, and church affiliations, creating a "social glue" that had held for decades if not centuries. Their network, over time, had developed an unwritten ethic for restoring their own particular watershed and foodshed.

It takes a village, I suppose. And the food and beverage producers themselves are not the only ones to benefit. So do at least four dozen species of breeding birds that depend on cottonwoods, willows, and the cool, shady pools of water below their canopies for foraging, roosting, and nesting.

In May 2017, I rolled up my blue jeans and waded down the stream channel of the Rio Sonora with ecologist Tom Sisk for four consecutive mornings just after dawn. There, in the cottonwoods and willow fencerows, we spotted rump-backed orioles, western kingbirds, vermilion flycatchers, ash-throated flycatchers, as well as several different tanagers, warblers, and thrashers. Wading in the pools beneath the shadows of the trees, we noted dippers, egrets, avocets, herons, and killdeer.

I was beginning to get the broader picture: Work together as a community to plant living fencerows. Let those planted willows and cottonwoods bring back soil and hold it in place.

Let those rich soils hold more water to protect the farmers' plantings from drought.

Let the nutrients in that deposited soil help grow both the crops themselves and shade-bearing trees that protect them from hot, dry winds.

And let the birds nest in these trees, where they can sally out over the fields and pluck insect pests out of the air.

Do you see what I mean? This effort by traditional farmers has built the kind of natural capital and ecosystem services that I refer to in shorthand as "food-producing capacity." That's what the farmers are after.

Seeing the birds in the trees or the hyphae on the root hairs in the soil is like icing on the cake. But what gets these Sonoran farmers up in the morning is the desire to keep their families fed.

They are wise enough to realize that their woven fencerows of willows and cottonwoods can restore their community's ability to produce nutritious food. It keeps them working next to one another, hand in hand, for something that truly represents *the common good*.

Whenever I think of that hackneyed term these days, I try to avoid abstractions. Instead, I look for a place where erosion is taking away the soil on which my neighbors and I once walked. We pick up some pruning shears and a shovel, find some mature cottonwoods or willows, prune their branches, and plant a little stretch of living fencerow there to hold the bank in place and accumulate more soil in front of it.

Each time it rains and floods, I go out to see whether there is more topsoil or whether it has eroded away. I watch to see if more of my neighbors can walk across it together rather than slipping into the gully.

That's one way I've come to value the common good.

CHAPTER 4

Replenishing Water and Wealth

Have you ever crossed a dry river bed at one point in your life, then come back years later to see its waters flowing wildly to the sea? Have you seen fish leaping above the waves, ducks diving into backwater ponds, wild rice cropping up along the river's edge, and dragonflies fluttering where they hadn't been for years?

As someone who has foraged or farmed, kept herds of sheep or flocks of turkeys in desert lands for half of my life, I suffer anxiety attacks whenever water is scarce. At the same time, I dream of bringing water back to habitats that have dried out over the past century. These fantasies are commonplace among those of us who live near the continental divide, between Rio Colorado to the west and the Rio Grande to the east.

The Rio Grande and Rio Colorado are the longest dewatered rivers in North America. For most of the last quarter century, their flows have barely made it to the oceans.

Up until 1998, the Rio Colorado could discharge as much as fourteen million acre-feet of fresh water into the Gulf of California, but now salty tailwaters from drainage canals are all that reach its delta.

While the Rio Grande can still discharge 1.7 million acre-feet into the Gulf of Mexico during the best of flood years, much of its midsection—from the Elephant Butte Reservoir in New Mexico to the Falcon Reservoir in South Texas—remains dry as a bone for months on end. My brother-in-law, who raises pecans in Pichacho, New Mexico, could once irrigate his trees eight times per season; today he is lucky if it's twice.

And yet these two "desert rivers" are not the only ones to see their waters dry up over the last century. According to surveys by the Environmental Protection Agency, at least 55 percent of US waterways appear to be in poor health. To be sure, nearly every river in the West is dotted with dams to irrigate farms and generate power, leaving long stretches of floodplain as barren sands or tangled banks of exotic salt cedars.

It is no wonder that so many species of native fish, freshwater clams, and migratory birds have seen their populations plummet. The birds depend on gallery forests of cottonwoods, sycamores, and willows, and those trees are disappearing. Not only is surface water scarce, but the underground flows that once moistened tree roots have been depleted by groundwater mining.

And yet even some of the most cynical environmentalists in North America now agree that we can reverse these trends, bringing fish back to swim and birds back to roost. As ecologist George Wuerthner recently concluded in the pages of the *Casper Star-Tribune*, "The dewatering of western rivers is not an accident. It is human caused—which means humans can fix it."

One of those humans is Valer Clark. Valer cofounded the Cuenca de los Ojos Foundation, building collaborations that have restored more than one hundred thousand acres of land along the US-Mexico border.

Valer does not do this work in a cultural or historical vacuum. She was well aware of Aldo Leopold's descriptions of ancient *trincheras* check dams, structures that actually return water to the landscape rather than diverting it. These check dams were built along mountain ridges in Mexico to slow floodwaters, capturing moisture and soil in land that would otherwise erode. In the 1940s, Leopold and his family watched deer browsing on the grassy benches held in place by check dams built centuries before on the Rio Gavilán, not far from Valer's own ranches near the Sonora-Chihuahua border.

She was also aware of the exceptional stonemasonry tradition in Guanajuato, Mexico, where *cantero* artisans have for decades built roadways, walls, and homes out of hand-cut caliche stone. She knew that in pueblos like Mineral de Pozos, this knowledge had been carefully passed from generation to generation. And so, in the 1990s, Valer began to recruit world-class stonemasons from Guanajuato to build check dams in the West Turkey Creek watershed near the Arizona–New Mexico border.

More than twenty years later, on a hot summer evening in June 2017, Valer led us down a trail to where some of the oldest dams still stood. Juan Olmedo, a Mexican agave farmer, and I were visiting her on El Coronado Ranch. I had stayed there for two days in the 1980s before she purchased it, when the land was virtually grassless due to years of neglect and overuse.

Not long after my first stay there, Valer and her partner at the time took over its management. Their vision for the ranch had a particular ecological precision, right down to the kinds of grasses, trees, and wildlife they wished to restore, including the then-endangered Gould's wild turkey.

As we followed Valer down the trail, we played the naturalist's game of "Name That Grass." It seemed there was a different species cropping up every few feet: deergrass, tanglehead, beardstem, several gramas, three-awn, and so on. I could hardly scribble their names into my notebook fast enough. At one point, Valer abandoned our guessing game and veered off the beaten path toward a canyon mouth. A side drainage ran down through oaks and pines from a ridge high above us. She signaled with a wave of her hand for us to follow.

Slight but steady on her feet, Valer headed down into the bottom of the watercourse and stood before a thirty-yard-long rock structure called a gabion, a special form of dry-stonemasonry check dam. Before we could catch up with her, she had disappeared around a curve, then reappeared beneath another giant stone check dam. Little more than five feet tall, Valer and her floppy hat barely rose above the top of the stone structure, built from hay-bale-sized boulders, some of them easily ten times her weight.

"Look here," Valer softly murmured, pointing to soil that rose five feet high at the base of the wall. It stretched out for another fifty feet before her. She held some of the moist soil in her hand. She explained that when her team began to restore the gully, the top of the check dam reached another five feet above her head. The land was little more than rocks and barren ground. But twenty years later, the soil had built up, along with moisture and grass.

"You know, when you want to make a difference, sometimes you have to begin with something big, *something bold*."

She went on with her story, walking before the dam as if on a stage. She told us that for the Guanajuato stonemasons, it was nothing to build dozens of check dams all the way up each of the side drainages, running to the top of the ridge.

"Dozens?" I asked, in awe of the amount of work it took to make just the one gabion immediately before me. "The *cantero* stonemasons constructed two or three dozen of these dams *per drainage*?"

"*More*," she said emphatically. "Maybe *eight to ten dozen* in each of the drainages."

But the structures didn't initially work as planned. A fire had left much of the ridge barren, with little besides charred trees. Every time a big rain came in the summer or fall, water and soil were flushed down the drainage, blowing out check dam after check dam. I had never heard about this setback. So I asked Valer how she had kept her faith up, how she kept going.

Her answer was simple. "Well, we just kept on repairing them, fortifying them." A few kept blowing out, but more and more of them held. Then in one big rain, char, blackened bark, and mud slowly filled in behind the check dams and stayed in place. It was like a big slicker slowly sinking in and locking things in place. Then the dirt started to build up and stay behind each dam, raising the level of soil by several feet each year. Pretty soon, the waters spread out across the entire canyon bottom. Gradually, a quarter-mile-long marsh developed where there used to be barren rock.

Juan and I were walking around as we listened to her, nudging our boot heels into the dirt, looking at its color and texture. We spotted the slick layer Valer referred to. But charcoal and microbe-rich soil were not the only things that the floods brought in. Valer waved us over to where she stood.

She pointed to sedges—water-loving plants—and a half dozen kinds of more mesic grasses. A few hundred sycamore tree seedlings stood before us. Valer and her team didn't plant them. The slowed-down flood-waters brought sycamore seeds, where they stayed and germinated. "Oh, and now we have frogs and toads arrive after big rains. And I just saw a heron catch one. Instantly the other toads dispersed, disappearing into the mud. I wonder how and what they were communicating to one another!" I wondered how the root communication network beneath our feet was working as well.

Juan Olmedo had been listening, looking around, and not saying too much as he took it all in. Finally he spoke up and asked Valer, "Do you have any idea of how many of these *trincheras* structures the *canteros* from Guanajuato have built on this entire ranch?"

Valer answered, "I'm not exactly sure. They've done thousands of these dams. I don't know . . . We stopped counting at twenty thousand." Valer may have stopped counting, but she has not stopped investing in restoring rich soil and fresh water. As she spoke, I realized that she regarded these resources as every person's birthright and the care of the land our collective responsibility.

Juan and I later learned that Valer was being rather modest in her estimate of how many *trincheras* check dams she has supported. When scientists with the Geological Survey inventoried them with remote sensing and follow-up walks to ground-truth their numbers, they discovered that more than forty thousand check dams had been put in place by the *canteros* of Guanajuato. They also found that 630 tons of moisture-holding soil were captured behind the dams in just three years.

One creek with a check dam had its flows during the rainy season reduced by half so that they were steadier, less flashy, and less capable of doing erosive damage. The restored creek was able to sustain at least 28 percent greater flow volume than a comparable creek bed that had not been restored. These stabilized flows ended up replenishing groundwater in the substrates below the check dams. Downstream, mile-long stretches are running year-round where they were once seasonally dry.

The check dams were sooner or later responsible for bringing back water striders, turtles, toads, frogs, fish, dippers, quail, coatimundis, and even large predatory cats. In fact, the quail on El Coronado help "pay" for the Cuenca de los Ojos investment in restoration work. Seasoned gamebird hunters pay thousands of dollars for a week in El Coronado's restored watershed, hunting three different species: Mearns's, Gambel's, and scaled quail.

Today, the children and grandchildren of the first *cantero* stone masons continue to build and occasionally repair the tens of thousands of check dams on the lands that Valer manages. It has become one of the most remarkable multigenerational, transborder collaborations ever accomplished in the *frontera* of Mexico and the US.

Valer sees her role in the project as one of catalyst. In her mind, she simply jumpstarted the ecological changes that will make the West Turkey Creek watershed increasingly productive for many more decades, well after Valer, the *canteros*, and the bird hunters are gone.

I've seldom heard a discouraging word from Valer's neighbors about the work that the *canteros* of Guanajuato have accomplished over the last few decades. If nearby ranchers have any reservation, it is that they themselves don't always have the money to similarly restore their own land's natural capital. Now that she has put livestock back on some of her restored lands, there is even more empathy among local ranchers for her efforts. Her healed land is yielding food again.

The only true gripe I've ever heard about the restoration work was not from her neighbors but from the US Border Patrol. Its administrators pouted for a while about how much water Valer's crew had brought back into the streams crossing the US-Mexico border. The steady flows were making it harder for their trucks to ford certain watercourses without getting stuck in the mud. The Border Patrol apparently liked it better when they could navigate dry, barren riverbeds that had not been restored!

I guess you could concede that one man's fish was another man's poison . . .

While Valer has invested serious capital in restoration, enormous sums of money are not necessarily required to change a landscape. Ranchers and range managers of lesser means are doing similar work—albeit on a different scale.

My favorite low-capital/high-impact builder of water wealth and soil fertility is Joe Quiroga, a hero of mine whom I've been blessed to live near twice in my life. Joe has been ranch foreman for the Jelks family on the Diamond C Ranch for most of the time I've known him and his wife, brothers, daughter-in-law, and grandkids.

Around the time that Joe turned sixty, he began an endeavor that has done more for land conservation than most of us will ever achieve. Having been temporarily relieved of managing the cattle on the Diamond C, he began to devote 100 percent of his time to managing the land itself.

One day, Joe looked out over the storm-scoured but dry watercourses of the Canelo Hills in Arizona's Santa Cruz County and decided that he would try to heal their wounds. He began to build a kind of stone check dam that looks slightly different from the *canteros' trincheras*. In fact, he began to construct them wherever he saw shallow waterways eroding into deep gullies, the chasms called arroyos in the Southwest borderlands.

Every week, year after year, Joe Quiroga rearranged the erratic boulders exposed in gullies or on the sides of ridges, moving dozens of them in order to span drainages.

Decades later, Joe can look out over the land and see the healing power of more than twelve hundred rock-solid check dams. He not only designed them but built them with boulders and cobbles he himself gathered. They have brought back steady stream flows and now hold hundreds of thousands of tons of soil and roots in place on the Diamond C Ranch—creating a little miracle of greenery in the otherwise cinnamon-colored Canelo Hills.

When I asked him why he had mounted such a herculean effort, Joe Quiroga offered me a simple, no-nonsense answer: "Because the land needed it."

"You know, building these check dams is a relatively easy thing, one that most anyone can do to help the land. I mean, sure, it's hard work, but it's the kind of work that nearly every one of us can achieve if we put our minds to it."

When men a half century younger than Joe ask this muscular seventy-five-year-old if he had any help moving boulders as big as whiskey barrels, he says, "Of course I did. Sure, I had a little help."

But then to their surprise, he casually mentions what kind of help: A digging bar. A pulley and ratchet that he hooks to the back of his pickup. And a bumper. Otherwise, this massive effort has been accomplished entirely by Joe's own two hands, his strong arms and sturdy legs, and his observant eyes, bright mind, and big heart.

"You know, all that is keeping any of us from doing our part in taking care of the land is some kind of tunnel vision. It blocks us from seeing that what we ourselves want for the land is more or less the same as what our neighbors want. That tunnel vision can paralyze us from taking action to do what virtually all of us would agree needs to be done."

Joe simply wants the land to be productive enough for his own descendants to make a living. Most of the Quiroga family has lived in Santa Cruz County for at least six generations, but some of the best and brightest of Joe's kin have recently left in search of decent jobs.

This lack of opportunity concerns Joe, who has been known to plaster various bumper stickers on his pickup truck—ones that express support for beef production and even mining. Those bumper stickers may irk environmentalists who pass Joe on the road, but he has a certain pragmatism that rings true to me. If land restoration and soil conservation can create enough jobs to keep his kids in the county, I'm sure he'd welcome those activities with open arms. But if it takes extractive industries to keep the twenty-first-century equivalent of brain drain from socially impoverishing his community, Joe simply will not disparage those pursuits.

And yet, Joe's own restorative work has been exemplary. The first year we took the Borderlands Earth Core youth out to see Joe's masterworks, his granddaughter Jodie was in our crew. She had never before seen the full extent of "water work" on the ranch, and the pride she felt for him shone through her beaming face.

Joe showed Jodie and the other teenagers how he had single-handedly returned running water and fertility to the floodplain in places that were formerly scoured clean. He showed them three-hundred-yard stretches of streams, gently flowing for the first time in decades, and a dozen native grass species providing perennial cover that may outlive all of us.

Around 1998, photographer Jay Dusard took a picture of Joe Quiroga along with Ruken Jelks II and Ruken Jelks III in a doorway of the Diamond C Ranch. The photo was featured in the fine book written by Dan Daggett, *Beyond the Rangeland Conflict: Toward a West That Works*.

In the pages of that book, I learned how one of my oldest friends, Tony Burgess, was once brought to the Diamond C Ranch during an era when environmental activists and ranchers were largely at odds with one another. By then Tony was a well-established desert ecologist who had helped design Biosphere Two and other world-class environmental projects. But when he looked out over a stretch of rangelands where Joe had increased the grass cover by 40 percent, Tony simply said, "I don't know what you are doing, but don't stop. It's working."

Two decades have passed since that incident, but Joe Quiroga has not yet stopped healing the land or divisions among people. On Earth Day 2012, more than seventy of his neighbors and a half dozen organizations—including farmers, ranchers, scientists, permaculturists, and community activists—came together to honor him at the Santa Cruz County Earth Fest.

Republicans, Democrats, Sagebrush Rebellion libertarians, and former Earth Firsters all paid homage to this homegrown hero, one who didn't readily fit any single label because he transcended them all. It was clear to everyone present that Joe Quiroga has left us a legacy that will live on for decades, if not centuries. Yes, it was Joe's patient day-by-day work that brought so many constituencies in the West to celebrate that legacy together.

Despite their cultural, political, and even economic differences, Joe Quiroga and Valer Clark share something special. They each take the long view of land health and have strived to make the world a greener, wetter place for all. They remind me of what Aldo Leopold first learned sixty years ago when he observed the abundance of moisture, soil, grass, and deer found behind the check dams built centuries earlier in the Rio Gavilán of Chihuahua: "I first clearly realized that the land is an organism [and] that in all my life [before coming to the borderlands] I had only seen sick land, whereas here was a biota still in perfect aboriginal health."

I hear the terms *environmental health* and *ecosystem services* bandied about these days, but people often forget that when Leopold first helped develop those concepts. The beneficial actions of land stewards from the border's many cultures were deeply embedded in Leopold's memory. Skeptics who believe that humans can only harm land and water—and never heal them—would do well to follow Joe Quiroga or Valer Clark out onto their lands.

More of us need to experience the lasting abundance that mortals like you and me can nurture within a lifetime. It's often hard to see how steadier, less erosive flow of water and more fertile pockets of soil translate into more food on the table and more money in the bank.

That's why I've been particularly inspired by Montana groups like Beartooth Capital, the Clark Fork Alliance, Montana Trout Unlimited, the Confederated Salish and Kootenai Tribes, and Trout Scapes River Restoration LLC. They have brought back not only streams but cutthroat, bull, and redband trout as well. The recovery of these edible fish has brought fly-fishers to rural communities and increased the value of any ranch where a trout stream runs. Beartooth Capital and its forty partners have completed thirty-four projects that have protected or restored thirty thousand acres on a dozen ranches, recovering trout populations along forty-five miles of slowly meandering watercourses.

A native cutthroat back in a healthy stream will eventually mean trout almondine in someone's frying pan.

CHAPTER 5

Bringing Back the Bison

Hᴀᴠᴇ ʏᴏᴜ ᴇᴠᴇʀ sᴛᴜᴍʙʟᴇᴅ ɪɴᴛᴏ ᴀ ᴘʟᴀᴄᴇ where you were bowled over by the astonishing abundance of wildlife?

Did your epiphany occur in the Pacific Northwest, along a river where wild salmon had begun their run upstream after months in the ocean?

Was it in the meadows around Horicon Marsh in Wisconsin or Bosque del Apache in New Mexico, where millions of geese and hundreds of cranes stop over each spring and fall?

Could it have been in the bayous of Louisiana, with Spanish moss dangling from the oak branches above you, while the waters beneath you swarm with freshwater shrimp, crayfish, gators, and all sorts of finfish?

And who were your companions on that day? Were there some folks you hardly knew before—Alaskan anglers, Spanish-speaking duck hunters, or Cajun crabbers and Creole chefs? Did they—like you—feel pulled to that place as if by some primordial force?

The overwhelming attraction was no magnetized piece of metal—it was the lure of life. More than two hundred and fifty species of delightfully wild animals are used as sources of food on the North America continent. They are also sources of wonder for the millions of Americans who take time to track these animals as the birds and fish make their annual migrations or simply move around their habitats. For many, myself included, it is a hope-renewing ritual to witness nature's bounty surge, sparkle, and swell before our very eyes each season.

In many cases, protecting these wild species simply means giving them enough open space to move freely. If we do not fragment or contaminate their habitats, they will do the rest. They already know how to live here.

This elegant message was recently brought home to me by a four-day visit with Hugh Fitzsimons on the Shape Ranch near Carrizo Springs, Texas. As Hugh and I bounced along and jawed in his little Kawasaki four-by-four, we followed a sandy track running through the scrublands of South Texas. While out and about, we stumbled onto a herd of more than eighty American bison lounging in and around a shallow laguna.

A rainbow hung over our shoulders that late afternoon as storm clouds rolled in from the Gulf Coast. The bison came running toward us (as if *we* were the attraction!), curious to see whether Hugh would be tossing out some snacks of cottonseed, mineral salts, and molasses for them. They closed in, most of them standing tall and shaggy, moaning and lowing with their deep baritone voices. Others, finishing a dip in the laguna, came running up to dry their shaggy black coats in the loose sand, dropping to their knees, then rolling on their backs, kicking up dust and shaping out shallow wallows on the sandy flats.

The bison had me mesmerized, but they were not the only performers that afternoon. A covey of bobwhite quail scurried past the Kawasaki on their way to thicker cover. At the water's edge, two white-tailed deer dipped their heads down to drink from the laguna, all the while watching us, ears straight up and alert to any sudden move that we might make.

Dozens of white-winged doves flew over us on their way to the water. Ducks and shorebirds kept their distance, staying out so far in the laguna that I couldn't confidently identify them to species.

"It's been at least a month since our last good rain," Hugh whispered to me. "No wonder they're all coming over to hover and huddle around the laguna."

On that particular afternoon and many others, water was indeed the true magnet for life in these parts. Life swirled around it, then came to partake of it. And "all" Hugh had to do was make sure that the water remained uncontaminated and accessible to life itself, on a piece of land large enough to offer forage, shade, and sanctuary: "Our philosophy is of minimal interference, allowing the bison to roam over thousands of acres of South Texas grassland, fattening themselves on native grasses and mesquite beans."

At one time or another, you have probably heard the numbers: twenty-four to thirty million bison (*Bos bison*) once roamed the grasslands and woodlands of North America. They were a most significant source of food for indigenous communities prior to the introduction of domesticated cattle (*Bos bos*), their closest kin in the Old World. But within a matter of decades, as wildlife historian Dale Lott has poetically put it, the population collapsed, falling from "thirty billion pounds of living, breathing bison-mass—to a carpet of whitening bones and a few hundred scattered survivors."

Those living, breathing, wildly roaming bison played no small role in nourishing the native inhabitants of North America's heartlands. Wildlife geographer Andrew Sansom has underscored their extraordinary role in shaping the American landscape:

"As the keystone species of North America's grasslands, . . . bison literally drove the biodiversity of the system. From the 100 million buffalo wallows that changed the hydrology of the plains and created habitat for wetland species, to massive impact on the plant communities, . . . the presence of bison was the principal causative factor at the landscape level . . . The profound ecosystem services provide by bison were enhanced by . . . Native Americans [who] set fire to the prairie in order to produce fresh forage for bison and other game. For centuries, this symbiosis of humanity and bison drove both the natural diversity and cultural heritage of the plains."

And yet overhunting, fragmented habitats, and diseases introduced from herds of cattle precipitated the near-extinction of both the sixteen to twenty million bison in the herds of the Northern Plains and the 8.5 million bison in the Southern Plains herd. The Southern Plains bison were smaller but more tolerant of heat, and they had somehow escaped much of the contamination with cattle genetics that befell the Northern Plains herd.

Notwithstanding, the Southern Plains herd was largely gone by 1879, except for five to seven individuals that legendary rancher Charlie Goodnight rescued and built to a herd of two hundred over the next half century. Fifteen more animals from the American Bison Society's Wichita Mountains Refuge were eventually folded in with Goodnight's herd.

After Goodnight died in Phoenix in 1929, his herd was in peril until it was bought by the Texas Game, Fish, and Oyster Commission in 1931. The survivors ultimately stayed put on Goodnight's ranch—the old JA—until they were transferred to Caprock Canyons State Park near Quitaque, Texas, in 1997.

When Hugh decided to purchase enough bison to build up a sizeable herd on the Shape Ranch near Carrizo Springs, Texas, few of the descendants of the original South Plains herd were accessible. Genetically unusual ones from the northern herd were also hard to come by. Hugh's vision of creating a free-ranging herd on private lands in South Texas was altogether different than what other Texan bison owners were doing at the time: "We wanted them to freely roam and forage just as they had for thousands of years. But at that moment in Texas, a few bison were being raised on private lands only as 'yard art' or for selling their calves into roping arenas for bulldogging events. They were being raised in miniature feed lots, not on the open range. In fact, that's what got me into it: looking into one of those feedlots and seeing that the spirit of the animal was dying under such conditions."

Hugh is correct that grass-fed, "free range" bison production has lagged behind that of cattle, sheep, and goats. In 2012, there were just nineteen certified grass-fed bison operations in the twelve Western states. By 2017, only six more ranches had been certified, edging the total up to twenty-five grass-fed sources in the Western US.

Still, there was the promise of some thirteen thousand acres of the Shape Ranch that Hugh's grandfather purchased back during the Dust Bowl, in 1932. It was available for a large-scale bison recovery effort, if he could just find enough animals to establish a diverse herd.

There were challenges. He had difficulty breeding the few animals he obtained that were descendants of Goodnight's legacy herd, but Hugh eventually found better breeding stock from Colorado, Utah, New Mexico, Oklahoma, and other states that he could integrate into his herd.

The Shape Ranch herd grew to be more than 250 bison before the 2011 drought forced Hugh to reduce its size by fifty so as not to overtax the land. Curiously, the herd stabilized at exactly the same size that Charlie Goodnight found he could manage over his years at the old JA Ranch in Palo Duro Canyon.

Under the conditions that Hugh offered them on the Shape Ranch, the bison were gradually selected for the very same characteristics that once made the Southern Plains herd so distinctive: shorter stature, lighter weights at maturity, few alleles from cattle genetics, and the ability to take the heat and humidity of more southerly climes.

As Hugh grew intent on learning more about best practices for bison management, he began to attend meetings of the Intertribal Buffalo Council (ITBC) whenever he and his ranch supervisor, Freddy Longoria, could get to them.

I myself had personally interacted with many of the tribal buffalo herd managers since 2005, around the time I joined my friend Kent Redford of the Wildlife Conservation Society at a "bison summit" in Denver. It was a retrospective of work done by many groups, including the American Bison Society established by William Hornaday a hundred years earlier. Around the time of that anniversary, Shawn Yannity, a leader of the Stillaguamish Tribe, put the growing Native American engagement in bison recovery into this culturally historic context: "Culturally, it's providing traditional foods of our ancestors and getting back to a traditional diet," Shawn explained. "The other part is continuing the traditions of using the whole animal for cultural uses."

Kent had invited me to the multicultural gathering in Denver to help facilitate one of the sessions dedicated to listening to the priorities expressed by various Native American bison managers. He wanted to ensure that their voices were a major part of the collective vision for bison recovery and prairie restoration in the Great Plains. Years later, I asked Kent why he made such a concerted effort to include the ITBC members as speakers and participants at that landmark meeting.

"Well," recalled Kent, "I just knew that you cannot and should not do anything without fully involving the original inhabitants of a landscape who are the original stewards of wildlife populations there."

Begun in 1990, the ITBC today involves fifty-eight tribes that cumulatively manage more than fifteen thousand bison in ways that nourish their culture and spirits as well as the ecology and economy of the region. But when Hugh and Freddy first attended as "listeners" at ITBC gatherings, this entire vision was still emerging.

"At first," Hugh confessed to me, "I just wasn't sure that we'd be welcomed or immediately accepted as participants at those meetings. I'm sure that some Native Americans must have initially looked at our presence with some skepticism, but we gradually made friends . . . and some of those guys generously took us in, sold or exchanged breeding stock with us, and taught me much of what I know today about bison. And I began to visit the Cheyenne up at Wind River, and Carl Tsosie up at Picuris in New Mexico, to see how they managed bison on their own reservations lands . . . Carl's Navajo and Pueblo kin are like family for me now."

Hugh wasn't simply trading information with the Native American bison producers; he was deepening the very way he thought about his endeavor on the Shape Ranch. Hugh began to gift bison-hair hides to the neighboring Kickapoo he knew from Eagle Pass, Texas, and Nacimiento, Coahuila, welcoming them to the ranch to gather some resources for their own ceremonies. And he also began to think about how bison and grass and water and mesquite fit into the restoration of whole landscapes.

That vision has extended beyond just taking care of his own private property to imagining how he might contribute to the ecological health of his Texas homeland: "Someday, I'd love to see a grass bank in this region that helps ranchers survive the droughts and that creates other sorts of jobs from the resources already here. I'd love to see bison being grazed on millions of acres of land that was restored and planted with Eastern gama grass. You know, you can still find some gama grass with roots up to twelve to fifteen feet deep. That's what we need: deep roots here."

Lest you presume that Fitzsimons cares about restoring land or recovering bison but not about reinvigorating regional economies, look again. His fresh, field-killed, grass-fed bison meat and bone marrow broth can be found in the Austin Farmers Market and in farm-to-table restaurants like Chef Elizabeth Johnson's PharmaTable in San Antonio. The hides are tanned. Wristbands are crafted from bison hide remnants. The wool is woven into blankets and rugs. And the short ribs are to die for . . .

But the Fitzsimons's vision for the land and the people of South Texas goes well beyond bison. Hugh is also collaborating with beekeepers to produce more honey from the guajillo, whitebrush, and mesquite trees on his land.

Hugh is now working with Dusty Crowe of the Natural Resource Conservation Service to see how mesquite pods might be ground into flour and sold as another regional product. And he has built roosts for wild turkeys, stocked his ponds with catfish and perch, and planted olive trees along the entranceway to his home on the ranch.

When I heard that he had been honored with the prestigious Gallo Gold Medal Award for the best artisanal food producer of 2007, I asked Hugh how he came to think of developing so many kinds of natural food products off the same land base. He just laughed.

"Oh, I'm perhaps the most backward kind of entrepreneur you can imagine. I find something that I remember that I loved during my childhood and then try to imagine a way to integrate an element of it into my present life."

When he paused for a moment, I realized that in his mind, he could fully *see* what he was about to recall to me. "There was this lady in Dilley Texas—my friend Todd's grandmother—that me and my father would always stop and see when we passed through her little town. She had this corner store where she'd sell these hard ribbon-like candies she'd made from the honey produced on the guajillo trees of our region . . . they were just so good . . . so memorable . . . that someday, years later, I just knew I had to do something to give the fine guajillo honey of my homeland greater recognition."

Hugh laughed again, at himself, I supposed. "To be sure, I'm not fully there yet in making it work as I hope it will. We've tried it once, and it didn't pan out, but this time I think we're collaborating with the right people. I have a feeling it's gonna work out this time. You know the flavor of guajillo honey, don't you? Make sure I send you home with a jar. And by the way, here's two Bison bars of soap I've been meaning to give you."

You could hear the mirth in Hugh's voice as he told me, "Now don't get me wrong, I'm not suggesting that you are exuding any particular offensive odor at this moment. But you just might want to use a Bison bar before you get home so that your wife can greet you with open arms."

What Fitzsimons has shown at Shape Ranch is that the production of healthy, delicious foods can go hand in hand with the recovery of wild biodiversity and the healing of cultural wounds. Those values are not inherently opposed to one another. In fact, they may be hitched at the hip.

Ultimately, they may also make for more robust local and regional food economies than those from which most Americans eat today. Within the last decade, roughly 450,000 bison have returned to the lands of the United States, Canada, and northern Mexico—about 95 percent of them on some 4,500 private and tribal farms and ranches in the three countries.

Only one in every eight bison of those herds—or fifty to sixty thousand animals—are processed each year at USDA inspected facilities. Another twenty to thirty thousand are annually processed in state- or tribe-inspected facilities. Since 2010, more than 7.5 million pounds of bison meat have been sold in the average year. That provides income not only to the 3,700 producers who sell their meat but to butchers and inspectors who work in more than one hundred facilities certified to capably and ethically handle bison.

Of course, not all of this meat is sold to and eaten outside of the bison producers' communities. Diane Amiotte-Seidl, a Native American health educator who has served as project director for ITBC, has found innovative ways to incorporate bison meat from tribal herds into the lunch menus of tribal schools and senior centers. "They sell the buffalo meat to the schools for the price of beef. The school turns around and pays the tribe to keep their herd going."

Those discounts are no small change, since the average pound of ground bison chuck retails in groceries for more than $10 a pound and strip steaks retail for more than $25 a pound. Nationwide, we're talking $100 to $200 million each year from bison meat sold in groceries alone, aside from the markup in restaurants and the donations or discounts that bring it into tribal cafeterias.

On the fifty-some Native American reservations where bison are raised, producers often "gift" healthy, grass-fed meat to their elderly in nursing homes and to youth involved in powwows. Others reserve their bison for ritual sacrifice at seasonal ceremonies out on the land itself.

But the most important thing to remember about bison recovery is that the most successful work has largely been done on private and tribal lands. In fact, about half of all the federally protected threatened and endangered wildlife species have at least 80 percent of their habitat on private lands. In a western state like Arizona where I live, a quarter of all undeveloped wildlife habitat is on tribal lands.

It has become increasingly evident to most conservation biologists that the full participation of private landowners and tribal land stewards is essential for the successful recovery of species such as bison, pronghorn antelope, sage-grouse, and wild turkey.

While several federal programs do provide incentives for private land-owners and tribes to conserve land, other USDA programs offer farmers far larger incentives to grow corn for ethanol production. These payouts are currently undermining the Conservation Reserve Program.

If the federal government continues to offer higher subsidies for corn than for conservation, both wildlife and eaters stand to lose. The US once had thirty-seven million acres under perennial cover on farms and ranches, but by 2017, that habitat had shrunk to just twenty-four million acres, a loss of 35 percent. What this implies, in essence, is that private and tribal landowners are preserving habitat for game, waterfowl, edible plants, and fish for reasons other than short-term economic gain.

They are holding on to the conservation value of their lands rather than selling it to the highest bidder.

And that decision, my friends, is one based on deeply American values: that sense of place matters, that open space matters, that free-ranging game matters, and that access to untrammeled lands for recreation or spiritual rejuvenation matters.

That the stewards of two-thirds of our once-thriving Conservation Reserve land base have stuck to their pledge to make room for bison and blue-winged teal, deer and mallard ducks, prairie chickens and peccaries, *despite* the economic pressures to do otherwise, says a lot. It says a lot about the tenaciousness of core values in America, values that bind us together with other species instead of letting them unravel.

CHAPTER 6

Teach a Community to Fish

Have you ever swept a net through a stream, a lake, or a river and found a fish you did not recognize?

Did you hold its wet, wriggling body in your hands, trying to decide whether it was edible, or so vulnerable to extinction that you should release it? After you tossed it back into the moving waters, did you wonder whether it survived or died, whether it reproduced, or whether it was eventually eaten by someone else?

Did the memory of that sleek, swift creature linger in the nerves and muscles of your fingers as if you had just had contact with something primordial?

I felt that way one day when we released several dozen fingerlings in the small reservoir below our home in the Sonoita Creek watershed. They were members of two rare native fish species struggling for survival, the desert pupfish and the Gila topminnow. Although both of these fish are too small to attract much interest from anglers today, they were in fact eaten by desert dwellers in past centuries.

With my wife and me that day were fisheries biologists from the US Fish and Wildlife Service and Arizona Game and Fish Department. Both agencies collaborate with private landowners to fund and implement the national Partners in Wildlife Program. But we also had with us Native American farming interns of Native Seeds/SEARCH, who were invited to ceremoniously release the fish into our pond. There were also ecologists from Borderlands Restoration Network and youth who worked with its Earth Care Youth Corps summer program to help the watershed above the reservoir hold onto more of its water.

Regrettably, fish species are not only threatened in landscapes like ours, where water is scarce. Today, 40 percent of all North American freshwater fish—those that have historically swam, fed, and bred in our continent's inland waters—are either imperiled or presumed already extinct.

The five-thousand-some freshwater fish of our continent once comprised *the* most diverse vertebrate fauna of any temperate region in the world but also the most endangered. Historically, we have not done well at sustaining the 435 fish that have been listed as threatened or endangered by the federal government, or the 72 additional species with distinctive populations that are also in trouble, and certainly not for the 36 that are already extinct in the wild. Most of those species were historically harvested for food, but overfishing has been but just one of many pressures propelling their populations toward extirpation.

A wide array of pressures are painfully evident along the 340 miles of Delaware River, the river upon whose shores I am sitting as I write up my field notes. It is the longest stretch of undammed stream on the Eastern Seaboard but also one of the most contaminated and deeply dredged. The Delaware once harbored millions of individuals of a peculiar fish that is seldom seen by anyone today.

That rare swimmer is the Atlantic sturgeon, *Acipenser oxyrinchus oxyrinchus*, one of two imperiled bonefish in these parts. They have wonderfully elongated bony-ridged backs that range in color from olive brown to dark blue, while their bellies are pale cream colored and smooth.

Even when put beside other *Acipenser* species, the sturgeon is a fish truly like no other. The Sturgeon General. The Philosopher Fish.

Reaching ages of sixty years or more, it is the longest-lived creature of its region, migrating from Delaware (and fifteen other rivers) into the vastness of the Atlantic all the way down to Cape Canaveral to the south and the Bay of Fundy to the north.

It is built like a tank, achieving the largest sizes of any fish in North America. Its massive bony-plated flanks reach lengths of fifteen feet—surpassing most bluefin tuna, sharks, and Colorado River pike minnow in length and girth.

This sturgeon species is extremely fecund. One sleek, ten-foot-long female hit by a tug a few years back was found to be gravid when her severed carcass was rescued by fisheries biologists. They took her back to the lab and estimated that the five-gallon bucket full of her rescued roe contained at least 2.2 million eggs. If those eggs had all hatched, they would have been sufficient to recover her species in one fell swoop.

And this sturgeon is certainly one of the oldest vertebrate species remaining on our continent. Dinosaurs, mammoths, and mastodons have come and gone, but the Sturgeon General remains in service, still in office. She carries in her seventy million years of knowing how to live in North American waters. All that wisdom is packed into her brain, her behavior, her oily flesh, and yes, her caviar as well.

Get into your own Wayback Machine and time travel just three centuries into colonial American history, and you will hear Thomas Harriot proclaim in 1580 that sturgeons were the dietary mainstay of many tribes he encountered along the Atlantic Seaboard. Harriot observed that "plentie of sturgeons" swam into every river in eastern North America, so much so that some Indian fishing villages brought in 58,000 pounds of their oil-rich meat per month.

Back then the "cows" regularly reached weights of 350 pounds each, 100 pounds of which were suitable for eating. The mature males and young "mammoses" were somewhat smaller, tipping the scales at one hundred pounds live, with sixty-five pounds of meat ready to eat.

And let me remind you that they were not only savored; they were also held sacred. First Nations fishers of Canada contend that there is no contradiction between needing a fish for nutritional sustenance and for spiritual sustenance.

Their passionate and persuasive argument has held sway in both provincial and federal courtrooms, assuring the fishers a portion of any sturgeon that migrate within their reach until this very day.

But let's step back from the shores for a moment. When John Nathan Cobb described the sturgeon fisheries of Delaware River and Bay in 1899, he made it clear that the Atlantic sturgeon were already in decline due to overfishing. (Most contamination came later.) Thousands of huge fish were still being harvested with gill nets and sold for their smoked meat, their oil, their hard caviar, and their value as fertilizer and as bait for eels and perch.

During that wrinkled moment in time, more than a thousand citizens of the Delaware watershed made their livelihoods off sturgeon. They labored as fishers, smokers, butchers, oil extractors, fishmongers, fertilizer hawkers, and bait shop managers.

Many of these commercial uses began along the Delaware in 1873 right where I sit, along the shores of Chester Creek, not far from where the Philadelphia International Airport sits today.

That's when a man named Henry Schacht began gillnetting where Chester and Ridley creeks flowed into the Delaware. He later took control of the now-vanished Monas Island in the Delaware, where he built underwater pens to hold huge captive sturgeon until market prices became favorable for their sale and slaughter.

Once caught and butchered, their bony bodies rendered roughly half their live weight in edible meat, caviar, and oil. As many as a thousand were hauled into a fishing village on a good day. Their migrations were blocked by dams and weirs, where they could be entangled in gill nets and stopped in their tracks. They were hauled up out of the water by heavy rope nooses slipped over their tails. They were speared with harpoons, gigged with hooks, trapped in dip nets, or wrestled to shore.

Even as Cobb shouted out his "red alert" about steep declines in the 1890s, there remained at least 180,000 individuals swimming in the Delaware River from spring to fall. A century later, less than a hundredth of that former number remained alive in the Delaware River and Bay.

Fisheries biologists like my friend Ian Park have worked long and hard to locate, catch, and release even seven hundred individuals per year in the Delaware, a number twice what the Delaware Riverkeepers had believed to be extant in the watershed. But the Riverkeepers' concerns remain valid: the sturgeon of the Delaware are in no way out of hot water yet.

The stretch of the Delaware where Ian and his crew monitor Atlantic sturgeon was finally declared critical habitat five years after the species was listed as endangered. But the fish still face a range of challenges, from dredging and blasting of the river channel to capture as bycatch in both US and Canadian waters.

In October 2017, Ian Park was kind enough to take me out on the Delaware to net, measure, and tag juvenile Atlantic sturgeon. It was a month before the blasting of the river's bedrock was to begin, deepening the channel so that larger ships could navigate it. Ian's crew members were intent on rescuing and later transplanting the sturgeon of Chester out of harm's way for a good reason. This reach was close to the highest known densities of juveniles anywhere in the Delaware, not far from the "safe harbor" known as the Marcus Hook Anchorage.

We met at a boat ramp in the midst of factories, oil refineries, sewage treatment plants, and soccer fields. Within an hour of setting out the gill nets and reeling them back in, we had caught four juveniles, all still short of celebrating their first birthdays. Their bodies were lanky but still less than nine inches in length. They had the five rows of bony scutes, the high ridge along their elongated backs, and the slightly upturned snout so emblematic of their kind.

"Look at this little beauty," Mike Steiger murmured as we worked together to gently liberate a seven-incher from the netting. "It's like a miniature of its parents . . . precisely the same shape and color."

As I took my first good look at an infant sturgeon, it seemed as though it was a beauty in the belly of the beast. It was starting its life in one of the most industrialized and contaminated rivers I had ever seen.

Now even those who dredge and blast the river bottom have been scurrying to work with biologists to reduce the hazards that have accumulated in the Delaware over a century or more.

To be sure, the fish are not the only lives to have suffered over decades of environmental degradation in this watershed. As the sturgeon dwindled with the contamination of the Delaware, the vitality of the towns and fishing wharfs on its shores has also dimmed.

Chester, Pennsylvania, today is a food desert, a factory town that has seen better days. Its Walmart, Family Dollar, Dollar Magic, and Dollar General stores still open their doors to cater to its poor, but many of its independently owned businesses have shut down for good.

Many of Chester's historic fish markets and seafood cafés have gone belly up just like the many fish species they once offered.

Despite daunting challenges, the communities along the Delaware have recently rallied to try to recover the Atlantic sturgeon, the river, and the local economies that once made them proud.

In particular, the William Penn Foundation's Delaware River Watershed Initiative set the stage for collaborative community-based conservation. Beginning around 2012, the Penn Foundation began to focus its environmental grant-making on the restoration of the Delaware, expanding its geographic reach to ensure that it could improve water quality throughout the entire watershed.

Since then it has offered an average of $30 million a year in new grants for research and advocacy, on-the-ground conservation and restoration, and community engagement. Through the fall of 2017, it has funded more than 130 different grantees for a total of $140 million. The goal is to build a broad constituency that is working to improve water quality and restore the watershed.

While the Penn Foundation program is not exactly focused on sturgeon per se, or even on biodiversity broadly speaking, its work has clear implications for any organism living in the river. By 2013, the Delaware River Restoration Fund was established to recruit additional donors to work in the region, including those who explicitly support aquatic habitat restoration and species protection. Some of this work uses funds funneled through the National Fish and Wildlife Foundation, with the Delaware River as a specific target. To date, these initiatives have eliminated more than two million pounds of nutrient loads and toxic sediments that were polluting the river and affecting sturgeon health and behavior.

Just how was this accomplished? With everyone rowing in the same direction! According to my contact at the Penn Foundation, Jamie Bartolino, "Collaboration and ground-up conservation approaches are the foundation of the initiative."

These collaborations now include more than sixty-five local, regional, and national partner organizations that have agreed to work together to restore wildlife habitat on land and the soil's capacity to hold moisture as well as to enhance water quality. The practitioners on these teams have been recruited from different local land trusts, Audubon Society chapters, Natural Conservancy reserves, and other community organizations whose work extends over a quarter of the entire watershed.

Remarkably, as the teams focused on protecting eight priority areas, they have affected surface and groundwater reserves that flow into the

Delaware from more than fifteen thousand acres of headwater forests. They have helped enhance the management on thousands of acres of farmlands as well.

What's more, they have restored habitats along miles of streams and hundreds of acres of wetlands. Sturgeon are not the only species to benefit from this restoration work. In fact, one key goal has been to make sure clean water is available to the fifteen million people in the Delaware watershed, many of whom live in some of the poorest towns and cities on the Eastern Seaboard.

As Jamie Bartolino explained to me about the Penn Foundation's Delaware Watershed Protection Program, "Protection of this resource is essential for the long-term health of these vulnerable communities, which have historically shouldered excessive environmental degradation and have not experienced the same level of access to the benefits of clean water as other communities."

As these efforts clean up the waters flowing into the Delaware, they will also improve spawning grounds. Biologists are now observing the first signs that the distinctive Atlantic sturgeon of the Delaware watershed are bouncing back from a historic low of three hundred or so mature females just a decade ago.

"What the new critical habitat designation for the sturgeon in the Delaware may bring," Ian Park explained to me, "is the opportunity to fully deal with the water quality problems that have been plaguing this place for a long time. The water quality in the river just hasn't changed all that much since the 1970s. This isn't just a sturgeon issue . . . It affects all species here."

Ultimately, watershed restoration and fish recovery must be seen as team sports and not the singular achievements of some lone star, a single community, or a single foundation. One coalition in the Delaware watershed—NJ Keep It Green—has brought together no fewer than 185 nonprofit, corporate, and agency members for its grassroots restoration efforts. Together, they have already protected 240,000 acres of farmlands, wet meadows, and woodlands in the watershed and are aiming to embrace another 800,000 acres.

These efforts not only create jobs. They also keep residents in the area talking and working together. Their benefits ripple out far beyond the fate of the watershed's most beleaguered fish. Some of those residents have recently rallied behind river restoration for an additional reason: social justice. They remember these words from Martin Luther King Jr.: "We are determined to work and fight . . . until justice runs down like water, and righteousness a mighty stream."

Let us pray that the Delaware once again becomes a mighty stream with a magnificent fish that can swim into its future as it did in its ancient history. And let us pray that the poorest people living along the shores of the Delaware thrive alongside the fish.

One thing has become clear, from the sluggish Delaware River clear to the desert streams and springs in the Southwest Borderlands: widespread restoration and recovery of fish species simply cannot and will not happen without significant investment in the kinds of community-based collaborations that have emerged over the last few decades.

Over fifteen years ago, Gary P. Garrett of a Fisheries Science Center in Ingram, Texas, realized that, while a quarter of the 170 freshwater fish in his state were threatened, they probably could not be saved without the on-ground cooperation of private landowners, private industries, and local agencies.

With the help of a half dozen scientists who were willing to change their approach from command-and-control to community-based fish recovery, Garrett changed the dynamic in Texas. He was able to bring in more than one hundred farmers, ranchers, water district managers, prison inmates, philanthropic foundations, university interns, and agencies to help with rare fish recovery.

Together, they worked to restore habitat for endangered pupfish and other species in West Texas, much like those in our little reservoir in southern Arizona. They have created new canals and basins and cleared out old structures of their invasive species.

To date, they have transplanted more than a dozen and a half species of native aquatic plants to provide food for the fish. Not only have the endangered fish begun to recover, but belted kingfishers, green herons, yellowthroats, blotched watersnakes, spiny soft-shelled turtles, and sliders have come to live in their restored ciénega habitats on their own accord.

Such work takes time—and patience. As Texas wildlife biologist Dusty Crowe once explained to me, "You have to set the table, then wait for the right moment to bring the diversity back."

That often means setting the right tone for collaborations like these to build confidence throughout the community, as Gary P. Garrett gradually learned. While each of the farmers was asked to give up a small amount of irrigation water to ensure the fish had an adequate habitat, they also wanted to see that future water supplies for their crops were guaranteed. In addition, the farmers requested that certain EPA regulations be relaxed so that they could strategically control the most troublesome insects and exotic weeds with highly regulated chemicals.

Garrett became struck by the fact that community members were working from more than self-interest—they really wanted to see the fish that they had helped protect.

Recovered populations of both the freshwater fish and marshland birds are now visible from an observation deck built by inmates from the Texas Department of Criminal Justice. There, as a grateful Gary P. Garrett has suggested, they can celebrate the fruits—and fish—of their shared labor: "Through a pragmatic understanding of the basic relationship between the natural and human communities, biologists and community leaders chose to work together on a solution that would benefit all concerned rather than adopt adversarial roles. While the farmers had previously viewed the fishes as something that hampered and perhaps threatened their livelihood, they realized the fishes could be their best insurance for sustained spring flows."

I'll second that emotion.

CHAPTER 7

Plant Midwives

Have you ever been hiking and stopped in your tracks to gaze at wildflowers so vibrant and abundant that you couldn't keep your eyes off of them? Did their delicate petals bring out the color in other lives found around you—the deer, the seed-eating sparrows, the other hikers making their way along the trail?

And was it just their beauty or also their scent—exuded for bees and butterflies—that told you that one day you too might taste this sweetness?

In late May 2017, ethnobotanist Joyce LeCompte offered me an opportunity to see such a sight and take a deep whiff of such a delectable fragrance. We hightailed it out of Seattle early one morning to rendezvous with others at the Glacial Heritage Reserve in the South Puget Sound area of western Washington.

There, the native plant in lavish bloom was the blue camas lily—*Camassia quamash*—the signature flower of wet prairie meadows in the Pacific Northwest. That spring, camas seemed to be blooming and blanketing the entire meadow in every direction we turned.

As far as our eyes could see, their six-petaled flowers added hues of pale lilac, violet blue, and deep purple to the vivid greens and subtle tans of the open prairie.

If you happened to arrive at the reserve unfamiliar with the restoration project happening there, you could easily assume that it was first and foremost about the restoration of *beauty*. After all, who could object to preserving the jaw-dropping, heart-pounding natural beauty of this world we live in?

The beauty of camas lilies was not ignored by previous generations of both residents in and travelers to western Washington. As early as the 1850s, camas lily bulbs were being dug up and shipped everywhere from the Atlantic seaboard to England to grace ornamental gardens.

But don't get me wrong; this camas lily is not just another pretty face to be sent off to Some Place Else. Its ultimate value may lie in its ability to combat adult-onset diabetes among the indigenous peoples of the Pacific Northwest. The complex carbohydrates in camas roots slow the digestion and absorption of glucose, flattening blood sugar levels and potentially reducing stress on the pancreas.

In addition to being a traditional food of great significance to First Nations communities along the Pacific North Rim, it may be a key factor in their future health. More than twenty indigenous cultures in western Canada and the US still tend, collect, clean, and pit-roast its bulbs for special seasonal events. Many of these communities hope that camas can help keep their children free of diabetes.

Of course, some of these intertribal "root festivals" have been taking place for centuries and millennia. But now, the bulbs are being dried and stored for families to eat year-round as one more means to deal with nutrition-related diseases.

Camas is just one of those "cultural keystone plants" that is both deeply intertwined with both indigenous health and the environmental health of the wet prairies. Thus the restoration of camas in wet prairies is linked to the restoration of human health for native communities who live in or near those landscapes.

And that is exactly why Joyce LeCompte of the University of Washington wrote an incubator grant to the Center for Creative Conservation: to bring together amazing women with diverse skills—Frederica Bowcutt (botany), Taylor Goforth (environmental communications), Valerie Segrest (native nutrition), and Sarah Hamman (restoration ecology). Their own goal was to provide technical as well as social support to leaders interested in camas that are emerging in Coastal Salish tribal communities.

The multicultural team set out to restore this landscape with the appreciation that indigenous knowledge, stewardship, and use of these plants matter deeply to neighboring communities.

I doubt that it has escaped your notice, but historically, most "environmental remediation" projects were dominated by men—albeit well-intended men—who inadvertently practiced a top-down management style that echoed the military as a whole and the Army Corps of Engineers in particular.

Under the auspices of "improving the environment" to control floods and stream flow, the Army Corps drained marshes and wet meadows while planting shrubs for game birds and to stabilize soil. That's exactly what plants like camas lilies do *not* need.

Few of these environmental engineers were even aware that local women were continuing to take their families out to harvest camas in places like the South Sound Prairies. As shrubs and Douglas firs moved in, camas lilies began to fade away, and harvesting became less frequent.

To reverse historic declines in camas and their traditional uses, Joyce and the other women who cohosted me have formed a multicultural "community of practice" for the edible plants and healing herbs of the South Sound Prairie.

I was heartened to see that these restoration and recovery efforts now involve dozens of indigenous harvesters, healers, and herbalists as well as land managers, botanists, wildlife biologists, fire ecologists, nutritional scientists, and ethnobotanical educators. They exemplify a trend that even the higher-ups in the US Forest Services now embrace: *that diverse membership in scientific communities fosters innovation and problem-solving more effectively than communities with a narrow range of knowledge, skills, and experience.*

In fact, many of the practitioners are women with a set of technical and experiential skills that ethnobotanist Kay Fowler calls "plant wifery." Elsewhere in the Pacific Northwest, ethnobotanist Madrona Murphy might be considered one of those "midwives." As she herself has documented, "Tribes cultivated [camas] in large gardens, subdivided into family-owned plots passed down through the generations. These were fertilized with seaweed, cleared of weeds and stones, and burned to control brush and grass."

Building on these ancient practices, the women in Joyce's entourage have initiated what they call "the Camas Prairie Cultural Ecosystems Incubator." They are like traditional midwives who use plants to help "bring out of the incubator" and into full light fresh ways of engaging with other people and with the land.

Together they have crafted a stunning vision statement: "Drawing on western and indigenous ways of knowing, this project will foster the health of Salish Sea prairies and the wellbeing of people connected to them, through collaborative partnerships based in trust, reciprocity, and respect."

As I watched this incubator team put their values into practice at the Glacial Heritage Reserve, I sensed that the women involved are *first and foremost attentive to camas itself.* They teach others that there is a culturally appropriate time to gather camas lily bulbs—when the lower half of the blossoms have begun to fade.

Some First Nations communities stay alert to when it is time to sustainably harvest the bulbs by what they call the "Camas Moon." They then begin to employ particular tools and techniques for gathering camas—ones that the "plant midwife" team demonstrated with their own digging sticks during our field trip.

When the digging is done properly, the bulbs pop out of the wet soil almost on their own. Historically, a knowledgeable camas digger could harvest as much as a bushel of bulbs a day from a gathering site of a half acre to an acre.

As some of these Coastal Salish restorationists already know, a traditionally managed gathering site should be cared for by clearing competing woody growth by hand or by burning, by replanting smaller bulbs, and by ensuring seasonal sheet flow of water across the site. They draw upon historic evidence that camas were grown by their ancestors in well-defined, meticulously cultivated populations that they tilled with digging sticks, hoed for weed control, and enhanced with bulbs they had collected from other nearby camas populations.

Patrick Dunn—the program director with the Center for Natural Lands Management—fully sanctions the use of these historic techniques and management strategies to bring camas back to their former abundance in the Glacial Heritage Natural Area. There, initial efforts have focused on reintroducing fire and engaging volunteers to thin invasive Douglas firs, which had grown up in the prairie during decades of fire suppression.

This particular restoration effort by the incubator team also has a social justice component. The program gets many of its native plants and seeds from inmates involved in the Sustainable Prisons Project, both reducing costs and building healthy relationships.

To be sure, the Camas Prairie Cultural Ecosystems Incubator team is also committed to human goals; they teach First Nations youth about the healing power and nutritional value of camas. A week after my visit to the camas prairie with Joyce, Sarah, Taylor, and Frederica, they hosted sixty tribal members from nine different tribes for both bulb harvesting and storytelling.

The community is now drawing on both traditional knowledge and Western scientific knowledge to tend camas and restore the land. But unlike in many cases, Western science is not privileged over local, indigenous ways of understanding. Both were welcomed. Even the divide between human and nonhuman nature has shifted.

In the welcoming space that the incubator team provided, some of the participants opened themselves up to different perspectives about plants and people. Is camas not "just" a plant but a sentient being and cultural ally as well? Are the traditional practices of harvesting camas merely "consumptive" or are they "regenerative"? Is wild plant restoration a "scientific management operation" or a "lifelong practice"?

Only when trust is gradually and respectfully built among cultures can such questions be fully explored and the challenges of collaborative conservation be fully addressed. And that is exactly what the Camas Prairie Cultural Ecosystems Incubator team of women has wisely and patiently chosen to foster.

More than eighty-two native species of once-declining food plants are being recovered through restoration projects in North America today—and many of the most successful efforts are led by women, especially women of color. Native American botanist and writer Robin Kimmerer has beautifully characterized the sensibility that they bring to such work:

"The people remaining on Earth must make a choice either to continue on the path that leads to destruction of life as we know it, or choose a different future—one of renewal. It is said that as the remaining people choose the path toward life, they will turn back along the road from which they have come and begin to pick up the pieces that have been scattered along the road—remnants of language, the old stories and songs, seeds and ragged patches of plants, wandering animals and birds, and collectively, they will put the world together again."

Of Anishinabe ancestry, Robin calls this process *reciprocal restoration*, for it is the "mutually-reinforcing restoration of land and culture, such that the repair of ecosystem services contributes to cultural revitalization, and renewal of culture promotes ecological integrity."

It is not surprising to me that women of color all over the world have taken the lead in building such reciprocities, especially in the collaborative practice of restoring habitats. Ghent University scholars Nicky Broeckhaven and Ann Cliquet have documented how gender equity can make ecological restoration more effective. Adding a diversity of perspectives—especially those of women from various backgrounds—to restoration initiatives fosters innovation both in research and in hands-on practice.

And yet, as Broeckhaven and Cliquet concede, a significant hurdle remains. It is "time to connect the dots" and fully empower women of all ages to play leadership roles in environmental stewardship and restoration.

Broeckhaven and Cliquet are not alone in their call. Even the World Bank, a notoriously top-down multinational organization, concedes that natural resource management is still too often dominated by men. The World Bank calls for rebalancing gender roles in fields such as ecological restoration and wild food plant recovery, noting that men have historically been the ones with more power, training, and access to technology. But for restoration to be successful, we need more equitable relationships among men and women (and the cultural groups they represent).

In short, our society can and must do more to ensure that women have an equal voice in ecological restoration, particularly women who understand the value of wild foods and the communities who depend on them. And frankly, as a male of Arab descent who was probably slow to fully fathom the significance of such issues, I no doubt missed out on a lot of learning.

In my own region, I must credit my colleagues Patty West, Teresa DeKoker, and Zsusi Kovacs—as well as my wife Laurie Monti and my old friend Shelly Silbert—with opening my eyes to methods of restoration that I never would have seen on my own.

In Flagstaff, Arizona, around 2002, Patty and I secured funding from the state to begin one of the country's first Community-Supported Wild Foraging (CSWF) projects, based loosely on the model of Community-Supported Agriculture. The year before, we had hosted a *wildly* successful community forum, in which we learned that $20 billion is spent each year on natural and organic foods, with wild foods gaining market shares in 130 countries around the world. Fiddleneck ferns, nettles, wild rice, ramps, prickly pear fruit, pinyon nuts, and other foods native to our area had made their way back into 73 percent of all the grocery stores in the US.

We were all aware that the Ecological Restoration Institute at our university, along with the US Forest Service and many other agencies and tribal governments, was ramping up efforts to restore ponderosa pine forests and pinyon-juniper woodlands in our region. Might we simultaneously harvest these foods while restoring forests on a large scale to reduce wildfire? Could "green jobs" for foragers be generated by an economic investment in restoration?

Even with such good intentions, our project initially got off to a rough start. Few of the land management agencies in our region were interested in opening public lands to foragers. Why? There was the knotty issue of potentially unsustainable harvesting that they had to deal with. My friend, botanist Lawrence Davis-Hollander, had already warned us that wild ramps (native onions) were being rapidly depleted in public lands on the East Coast because of soaring market demand. Word of this problem had spread like wildfire among public lands managers.

Lawrence and others estimated that between eighteen thousand and twenty thousand pounds of the onions were being extracted from wildlands each year for use in New York City restaurants and markets. Overharvesting had spiked their prices as high as $12 per pound! The Forest

Service botanists we initially spoke with did not want any part in letting foragers loose on public lands to harvest plants for profit. Land managers were not enthused.

But while I was trying to figure out ways to defend our original plan to agency bureaucrats, Patty West took another tract that proved far more successful. Patty proposed that we gather invasives—the berries, seeds, shoots, roots, and fruits of edible plants that had been accidentally introduced to forest lands. These included Siberian blackberries, horseradish, tumbleweed, watercress, dandelions, and the like. She worked up a broader list and presented it to the Forest Service.

The answer from Forest Service scientists? *Go for it, Patty.* They were happy for us to not only "weed" out the invasive plants but also gather nonnative crayfish and bullfrogs. They would even give us locations where they wanted species reduced in order to recover more native species in restored habitats.

By the time Patty West and Teresa DeKoker received all the permits, maps, volunteer foragers, and paying shareholders to move the project forward, they had a plan for delivering fifty-six wild products to twenty-three households and several restaurants over a fifteen-week season. They also sold wild exotic foods through the Flagstaff Community Farmer's Market and contacts with local chefs.

Soon we were organizing and celebrating a new seasonal event—the Flagstaff Foraged Feast—that offered samples of dozens of wild foods to more than two hundred residents. The project and the celebration continued to morph for several more years after state funding ended, and the Foraged Feast is still alive and well.

Patty West, the real "local hero" behind this foodshed restoration initiative, later summed up the effort in this manner: "We provided short-term [seasonal] jobs for rural residents . . . Our sales and educational booths at regional festivals and community fairs impacted over 1,000 people. We were featured by reporters on local radio and in regional newspapers, but news of the project went viral and was eventually covered by a *National Public Radio* program, *Gourmet* magazine, and *High Country News*. Finally, we developed a manual to help others start restorations projects like this in their own areas."

Patty and Teresa trained dozens of volunteers how to forage ethically, in ways that were ecologically responsible but fun too, building community as they went. I could never have engaged as many chefs, backyard fermentation experts, herbalists, forest ecologists, restoration activists, and Native American healers as they did.

For me, the real hallmark of their genius came when they joined forces with the Grand Canyon Wildlands Council. Together, they removed introduced crawdads and bullfrogs from Beaver Creek and put them in the hands of Slow Food chefs who cooked up New Orleans–style gumbos and frog legs. More than fifty participants sat and enjoyed these foraged delicacies as Cajun musicians entertained us—all in the very forest that was being restored. That, my friends, is conservation that you can not only taste but sing along to as well.

CHAPTER 8

Strange Birds Flock Together

Have you ever walked out from a farmhouse in the morning to listen to a herd of cattle lowing in the pasture or a clutch of chickens clucking and scratching as they strutted around their pens? Did they somehow *call out to you* as if they were part and parcel of your primordial past and might be linked to your future?

I felt that way the first summer I worked on Pleasant Valley Farm, an interracial, multicultural camp in Woodstock, Illinois. The camp engaged youth groups, handicapped adults, and immigrant families in agriculture and ecological restoration.

It was a program of the Community Renewal Society, a nonprofit that served the urban poor throughout Chicagoland. There, all could hear the gobbles and grunts, the cackles and clucks, the bleats and brays from the menagerie as soon as we awakened in the morning.

Even though I had grown up in the barely arable Indiana Dunes, these barnyard sounds felt deeply familiar, as if they had thrummed and echoed through the veins of my own ancestors.

As an environmental educator at Pleasant Valley, I helped the resident farmer knock off a few barnyard chores now and then, but I also pitched in to milk the Mason family's goats whenever I could. Here was something deeply satisfying about helping others with such work, whether they were Anglo-, African-, Latino-, Asian- or Native American.

Later, when I tended to my own herd of Navajo-Churro sheep and a flock of standard-breed turkeys, I began to collaborate with rural people whose cultural backgrounds were far different from my own urban upbringing: Navajo, Hopi, and Hispanic families who had always made sheep and turkeys part of their lives.

One Navajo herder named Leon Tsosie showed up at our corrals to purchase a couple Churro ewes and a ram and ended up living with us for four years running. He taught me how to tend to these animals—predator-proofing fences, shearing the sheep's fleeces, and butchering their meats—in ways I could have hardly learned on my own.

While our friendship deepened, another perhaps more remarkable one was emerging between two men who lived far to the east of us. The two could not have been more different in their upbringings, politics, environments, access to resources, or professional training. But their friendship became evidence that we can bridge America's urban-rural divide—and bring back the rich diversity of our foods in the process.

When Frank Reese Jr. of Lindborg, Kansas, and Patrick Martins of Brooklyn, New York, met in 2002, America's poultry breeds seemed to be in trouble. At the time, just five livestock slaughtering, processing, and packaging companies controlled 78 percent of the meats bought and eaten in the US marketplace. Those five companies held sway over the meat buyers for the top ten grocery chains and the top ten fast food chains on the continent.

Just four commercial poultry breeders monopolized 95 percent of all the turkey in the country, and they exclusively offered just one lineage, the highly uniform Broad-Breasted White turkey. Most home cooks at that time knew their turkeys only by the names Butterball or Jenny-O and could not even recognize the particular breed they were feeding their families on Thanksgiving or Christmas. For them, a turkey was a turkey was a turkey. Reese and Martins somehow changed all that. But when their collaboration began, just a few birds of different feathers were left in farm country, and few of us were even tasting or seeing them.

Born in 1948, Frank R. Reese Jr. had lived most of his life as one of three thousand citizens of Lindborg, a prairie town in the red county of McPherson in the red state of Kansas. It's a place where conservative Republicans have won most elections in recent decades. Roughly 95 percent of his neighbors are classified as white, and the majority of those are of Swedish descent. And yet such statistics hardly describe the full range of cultural influences that have shaped Frank Reese Jr.

Raised on a farm that has been in his family for upwards of a century, Frank was mentored from age six onward by some of the greatest old-timey poultry breeders in America's honey-colored heartland. When he was in first grade, he saw a flock of twenty thousand Bronze turkeys belonging to Verle and Agnes Trow. He fell head over heels in love with turkeys and never ever recovered.

Frank began raising standard breeds of turkeys in 4-H clubs by the time he was eight, walking them out into pastures to eat grasshoppers during the day and letting them follow him back into the pen before sunset. Later, Norman Kardosh, "the Turkey Man of the Midwest," taught Frank how to select turkeys for their conformation and breeding ability and not just for their plumage color and size.

Frank had a knack for science and was trained as an anesthesiologist—a profession he still practices part-time today. He worked in South Texas hospitals for a while before returning to Kansas to become the fourth generation of Reeses that farmed in McPherson County.

A self-described introvert, Frank Reese became a good listener, observer, and rigorous defender of agrarian traditions. When I walked with him around his turkey pens at Good Shepherd Farm in the autumn of 2017, it seemed as though at every step, he was guided by the invisible presence of turkey-breeding elders, ancients, and angels: Norman

Kardosh, Sadie Lloyd, Ty Patton, Agnes Trow, Bill Crawley, and George Nicholas.

Frank told me of the very values that these mentors had imparted to him: "George Nicholas once explained to me that you don't ever want to get rid of any of the key assets that have been fundamental to turkey breeding over the decades . . . And so I hold on to key traits in my breeding stock and make notes on how each of them can be potentially useful to a turkey producer. And for that reason, I also remain very farm-oriented. That's because I deeply care that the farmer can still make a living raising turkeys by having something unique to offer the chefs and consumers."

He paused and then added, "And yet so many of the pieces that once made turkey raising profitable are now missing. Farmers can't do it all by themselves anymore. You can't work alone, you have to make alliances."

Frank was silent for a moment. I asked if he was referring to the kind of alliance he had forged with our mutual friend, Patrick Martins, cofounder of Heritage Foods USA. He nodded.

"Yes, and that's exactly why Patrick Martins is one of my heroes. I would do anything for that man because he has consistently shown that he will do anything for me. Oh, you know how Patrick is. To the unacquainted, he might come across to some as a rough and tough wheeler-dealer from Brooklyn, but he always holds true to what he says he will do. He's proved himself to me so many times . . . including saving my butt once when I nearly lost the whole works, turkeys and all. Patrick is unique among buyers of heritage meats, for he's never crossed the line by pressuring me to do something that might undermine my values."

Enter Patrick Martins from stage right on the East Coast. Born in 1972 in Mount Sinai Hospital in New York, Patrick Martins has lived much of his life in and near Brooklyn, notwithstanding his brief but formative residencies in Italy. It was there that he became acquainted with the leaders of the international Slow Food movement, who encouraged him to serve as the founding director of Slow Food USA.

Patrick would be the first to admit that he had grown up without ever raising or butchering a turkey. Nonetheless, he developed a keen interest in securing the legacy of this iconic American bird.

At first glance, his professional training didn't seem to prepare him for the conservation of rare breeds or the promotion of heritage meats. His master's degree from New York University's Tisch School of the Arts was in performance studies, not animal husbandry. And he was the creator of the New York City Trivia Game, not a bird breeder in Carhart overalls and Red Wing boots.

In 2001, after talking with Frank and the staff of the American Livestock Conservancy (ALBC), Patrick came up with somewhat of a "publicity stunt" to draw attention to rare turkeys. At Thanksgiving, Slow Food USA's national office would sell breeds that had recently been on "the Ark of Taste," an international catalog of endangered heritage foods. When he had searched for sources with enough birds to sell for Thanksgiving dinners, he realized that Frank's Good Shepherd Farm was essential to any recovery of America's turkey heritage. Frank had lines of genetics that could be traced back 150 years to the preindustrial era.

"You see," Frank explained to me as the Bourbon Reds and Bronzes huddled around us in his turkey yard. "You can't get out of factory farming by trying to make a silk purse out of a pig's ear. What I mean is that if your free-range, pasture-fed, organic birds have industrially selected genetics, you just can't get to where you want to be. If the genetics of your flock is bad to begin with, nothing in your organic feed can make up for that."

In advance of their first Thanksgiving promotion, Frank raised nine hundred birds of impeccable lineages to sell through Patrick's network. By the next Thanksgiving, Frank had another 1,600 ready to go, and Patrick was fully ready to place them.

And then news of their efforts went viral, and demand leapt far ahead of supply. Martins left Slow Food USA to found Heritage Foods USA and immediately recruited Frank to be a "founding producer." In no time, Frank mobilized to raise and sell as many as ten thousand turkeys, hens, ducks, and geese a year through Patrick's supply chain. His birds were soon found in the capable hands of more than 130 chefs at work in cutting-edge restaurants in all fifty states.

Not mild-mannered, keep-your-secret-ingredients-to-yourself chefs, mind you. Controversial chefs like New York's massive personality Mario Batali, who shouted out this message: "These birds are without a doubt the *tastiest birds you can possibly serve*. I've served these birds for my Thanksgiving every year for the past twelve years and always will."

Molto Mario was not the only chef to vote with his checkbook for Frank's birds. Frank's turkeys also got a nod from charismatic, game-changing West Coast chefs like Alice Waters at Chez Panisse in Berkeley. And other high-profile chefs weighed in too, ones who had heard of the American Livestock Breeds Conservancy but weren't initially sure that it was a good idea to tell their customers that they would be tasting endangered birds. Chefs who, with the likes of Frank and Patrick, became ready, willing, and able to use these birds to bridge the urban-rural divide.

Let's pause for a moment to consider some history, for this collaboration of strange allies catalyzed an enormous effort to recover rare turkey breeds in the blink of an eye. In 1997—the very same year I first raised a few of my own Black Spanish and Bronze turkeys in southern Arizona—there were only 1,335 breeding hens remaining of the rare breeds of turkeys known to have developed on American soil.

By 2006, the number of breeding hens had jumped up to 10,404. By 2015, their numbers had reached 14,502, eleven times the population eighteen years earlier. Today, there are at least 30,000 individual birds of a full dozen standard or heritage breeds out on American farms. While Frank was a leader among the twenty-eight "heritage" or "standard" turkey breeders left in America when these efforts began, there are now more than six hundred such turkey breeders active in nineteen states.

All told, Frank and Patrick helped recover eight of America's rarest poultry breeds, bringing them back from a critically threatened status. They are but two of thousands of conservationists who now work to maintain poultry diversity. In fact, forty-two of the eighty-one varieties of poultry (of all species) that are the rarest in America in 2000 have seen astonishing recovery over the last two decades.

Curiously, most breeders of rare standard breeds of turkeys live and work in the so-called red states—the presumed bastions of fiscal conservatism, private property rights, and antienvironmentalism. But don't assume that these fiscal conservatives only care about lowering taxes and driving up their profits from private land deals or you will be in for a surprise. The most successful reintroductions of wild turkeys and restoration of their natural habitats have occurred in red states, where generous investments have bolstered populations on both public and private lands.

When the National Wild Turkey Federation featured what it believed were the biggest successes in habitat restoration for wild turkeys, six of the most celebrated initiatives occurred in red states, while two occurred in blue states. So it seems that turkeys know how to walk across the aisle and fly in the face of hardliners on either side, transcending politics to inspire us all.

And Frank Reese Jr., a lifelong rural resident of red states—Kansas and Texas—has also learned to walk across the aisle between rural and urban, conservative and liberal, Democrat and Republican, black and white, in a manner that few Americans of his era fully embrace. Just before I left Good Shepherd Farm, Frank invited my friend Aubrey Krug and me into his dining room. As Aubrey and I sat across the table from him, I could see a large painting of *The Last Supper* over one of his shoulders.

Oh yeah, I thought to myself, *Good Shepherd Farm . . .*

Gil Waldkoening, a professor of church and society at the Lutheran Theological Seminary, has called such farms "the scenes of grace" in the ecological restoration movement.

They are places where people of various faiths both care for Creation through their daily activities and begin to heal old wounds. They are not only *restoring* the land and its biodiversity but *restorying* our human relationship with creation, in ways that may change behaviors, patterns of consumption, and our openness to others.

I felt that I could not leave Good Shepherd Farm without asking Frank if his faith affected his willingness to work with so many kinds of people as well as so many different breeds of poultry. He answered my question nonchalantly: "Well, I try to pitch in where and when I can."

Since 2015, Frank has been working with Kansas Wesleyan, a United Methodist–affiliated college up the road at Salina, on the development of the Good Shepherd Institute. The nonprofit will teach agricultural experts, farmers, and students about techniques for preserving rare and heritage livestock.

In the fall of 2017, at the age of sixty-seven, Frank was tending thousands of turkeys while still working as an anesthesiologist and, on the side, creating a groundbreaking institute. Before I had time to really ponder all that he was accomplishing, his face lit up as he mentioned one more project.

Frank had begun working with an interfaith group in Kansas City called the Mighty Men of Valor. The organization helps Christian men of all races and church affiliations to overcome their addictions and become leaders in their communities. "Can you believe it?" Frank asked with his characteristic humility. "They seem to be interested in what I'm trying to do here."

I looked over at Aubrey, and we were both grinning. *Yes, we can believe that.* Around Frank, it seems that anything is possible . . .

Fortunately, Frank Reese Jr. has inspired many others to jump into the dance of recovering rare poultry breeds. Although he remains among the most skilled breeders working today, he is no longer alone in such efforts. The American Livestock Conservancy recorded no fewer than 1,500 private poultry breeders, 48 hatcheries, and 7 universities now engaged in the recovery of these rare birds.

When the Conservancy conducted its Great American Poultry Census in 2015 and 2016, it found that rebuilding this support network had enabled more than four million poultry enthusiasts who are engaged in raising turkeys, ducks, geese, and chickens of distinctive breeds. Among the eighty-one rarest poultry breeds in North America, 26 percent of the rare breeds of turkeys are more numerous than when last counted between 2000 and 2006.

Remarkably, more than half of all those rare poultry breeds are now represented by more than a thousand breeding birds, making them far more secure than reflected in the previous censuses. Seven of the breeds are represented by more than five thousand breeding birds, which means they are getting close to full recovery.

After fewer than fifteen years of bringing these birds back from the brink of extinction, fifteen chicken breeds, five duck breeds, three goose breeds, and one turkey breed are more secure than they have been any time since World War II. However, it would be missing the point to think that these herculean efforts are merely about the "genetic recovery" of poultry antiquities that have been dismissed as "obsolete" since they hold no sweet spot in the current American marketplace.

Today, you can find more than a thousand producers who market the eggs and meat of formerly threatened poultry breeds through independently owned restaurants and charcuteries: Buckeye, Delaware, Dominique, Java, and New Hampshire chickens; Cayuga ducks; Cotton Patch geese; and American Bronze, Black Spanish, Bourbon Red, Narragansett, and Slate turkeys.

Patrick Martins of Heritage Foods USA has argued that rural breeders could not have accomplished such a rapid recovery of these rare breeds were it not for urban chefs who were immediately willing to pay a fixed price per pound of meat—often in advance—to the farmers themselves: "The chefs have really rallied behind the notion of restaurant-supported agriculture. They have helped maintain a beautiful landscape all across America."

I was struck by the ethical underpinnings of Patrick's words. A bridge between rural and urban peoples, who (re)discover the values they hold in common while working together to defend rare breeds and to make our shared landscapes more beautiful.

Something that might be dismissed as trivial—reviving the likes of rare domestic poultry breeds—has now created a movement that honors this modest portion of Creation. From this "safe nest," phoenixes are arising from the ashes to live among us once more.

CHAPTER 9

Herders of Many Cultures

Have you ever seen sheep vault a fence, unperturbed by the barriers we think will hem them in? Have you been stunned by their grace and agility—as if they were four-legged ballerinas practicing their arabesque positions without regard for the hazards of their studio?

I had such a feeling overwhelm me once as I tended our flock of Navajo-Churro sheep in the volcanic badlands stretching between northern Arizona and New Mexico, near Diné (or Navajo) Nation lands.

One by one, then three by three, Churro ewes and spring lambs leapt over a low, zigzagging fence of cedar logs that edged our property. It was lovely to see our twenty sheep move instinctively like fish in a school, pivoting, running, and leaping over the thirty-inch snow fence, then hustling up the mesa toward a gate into the pine forest.

I followed along behind them with my wooden shepherd's staff, hoping to give them some real exercise before a snowstorm came in that would keep them in their pen for at least a couple days. But tending the sheep offered me real exercise—both physical and mental—as well.

Those eight years of counting sheep, along with two brief years serving on the board of the Navajo-Churro Sheep Association, were as close as I ever came to being a stockman, sheepherder, or rancher.

I learned from my neighbors how to assist our ewes with their lambing, to shear and wash their wool for my wife Laurie to spin, and to butcher their meat for sharing at communal feasts with our Navajo and Hopi friends. But I also was humbled to concede that I did not have skills, the access to sufficient pastureland, or the perspicacity to make a living as a sheep producer.

Instead of being discouraged, I simply became more thankful for those around me who had the tenacity to do it right. A number of Diné sheepherders and weavers—from Leon Tsosie and Roy Kady to Colleen Biakeddy, Jones Benally, Virginia Herder, and her daughters—have enriched our lives in innumerable ways.

So have Hispanic sheepherders like Antonio and Molly Manzanares, who market much of their Shepherd's Lamb in Santa Fe while living on a two-hundred-acre ranch in the Chama Valley near Los Ojos, New Mexico.

As I have been instructed in the ways of sheepherding by these patient friends over the last two decades, I have learned things—not just skills, but values as well—that I regret not having learned from my Syrian grandfather, Papa John Nabhan, who herded sheep before being forced to leave his homeland near the present-day Syria-Lebanon border.

But I also learned how tough it can be for any small shareholder to make a living raising sheep or goats, cattle or bison in this day and age, when virtually all market forces seem to be working against you.

And yet small shareholders—whether nomadic herders or stockmen who keep their flocks in the same irrigated pastures year-round—remain the lifeline for most of the rare livestock breeds left in North America. Nearly one hundred distinct breeds that declined over the last century are now being revived by small shareholders.

My colleagues at the American Livestock Conservancy maintain a Conservation Priority list of rare breeds, which they periodically update to determine whether each is moving toward full recovery or moving in the other direction, toward critically endangered or threatened status.

As of 2016, the organization remains concerned about twenty-two breeds of cattle, twenty-two breeds of sheep, twenty-two breeds of horses (including seven distinct strains of Spanish and Indian mustangs), twelve breeds of rabbits, ten breeds of pigs, six breeds of goats, and three breeds of donkeys.

Roughly a third of those breeds—thirty-one out of ninety-seven distinctive livestock lineages—are critically endangered. Another thirty breeds are threatened, as is every strain of Spanish and Indian mustangs. Navajo-Churro sheep, the breed that Laurie and I tended, are one of those thirty still considered to be threatened.

You might ask why such a high percentage of livestock breeds are threatened compared to poultry breeds or even crop plants. Well, for starters, they live longer and have fewer offspring. In addition, it's a lot harder to keep sheep or cattle in your backyard than turkeys or heirloom tomatoes.

Navajo-Churro sheep populations plummeted because of changing global market trends and because the federal government pursued eradication policies of breeds perceived to be "unproductive" and "unmarketable" over the last century.

By the late 1970s, there were only 450 purebred individuals of this historically important Churro breed. The sheep appeared on the brink of extinction—as did, amazingly, a full third of all livestock breeds in the world at that time.

You could not find Churro lamb on a restaurant menu anywhere in the US, and neither their meat nor their wool was differentiated from others in the marketplace, so they garnered the lowest commodity prices.

But then something remarkable began to happen. A collaboration began around 1977 between an Anglo livestock scientist of Scottish descent, Lyle McNeal, a dozen Diné families (including the Begay, Bluehouse, Wauneka, and Kady clans) and a dozen or so Hispanic families (including the Manzanares, Martinez, and Salazar clans).

They established the Navajo-Churro Sheep Project to rescue the few purebred rams and ewes left for restoration breeding. Other talented individuals—from MacArthur Award–winning community development activist Maria Varela to pioneer Churro promoter Ingrid Painter to breed registry curator Connie Taylor—also volunteered their time.

In the early 1980s, a number of these individuals and families began to get together for occasional exchanges of breeding rams and information in Farmington, Ganado, and Los Ojos—small towns not far from the New Mexico–Arizona border.

It was around this time that I saw my first Churros. I was struck by the colors of their fleeces, by the rare individuals that sported four horns, and by their alert and inquisitive nature.

They were beautiful to my eye. I was hooked on trying to help them in some modest way myself. So I suggested to the Phoenix Zoo, where I was volunteering as a science and conservation advisor, that they both get involved in conservation breeding and keep Churros on their grounds in Papago Park, Arizona.

About that time—1986—one of the Southwest gatherings led to the formation of the national Navajo-Churro Sheep Association. The placing of that hyphen in the association's name, by the way, was a conscious decision of those who met in Los Ojos to not only incorporate a new nonprofit but to do it in a multicultural manner.

This breed had four hundred years of history with Spanish-speaking herders in New Mexico and a relationship with the Diné, several Puebloan tribes in New Mexico, and the Hopi for nearly that long.

To explicitly declare that this breed was linked to the heritage of both Hispanic and Native American communities was no small gesture. In fact, that is also why the first board of the association had copresidents: Antonio Manzanares of the Hispanic community of Tierra Amarilla, New Mexico, and Milton Bluehouse of the Diné community of Ganado, Arizona.

And for anyone who might assume that Anglos were left out, nothing could be further from the truth. To this day, Lyle and Nancy McNeal, as well as registry hosts Connie and Sam Taylor, are revered by many of the founding Diné and Hispanic families in the association.

Once, when I brought the McNeals into Flagstaff, Arizona, for a presentation on their collaborative work with the Navajo-Churro Sheep Project, a half dozen Diné families drove for more than a hundred miles to set up camp below the stairs of the auditorium where Lyle was to speak. They brought hand-spun wool and finished blankets to gift the McNeals and plenty of lamb stew for the rest of us to savor!

Now let me just cut to the chase: by 2005, these collaborations had increased the total number of breed-registered Navajo-Churro animals to more than 5,500, eleven times the count when they were at their all-time low in the 1970s.

As of 2017, that number had risen to 7,600. Connie Taylor, who continues to manage the Churro registry for a third decade, estimates that at any given moment, between lambing and butchering cycles, at least 5,000 Navajo-Churro sheep are being pastured.

The delicious, grass-fed lamb and mutton meat from this breed is now in restaurants in the Southwest every week of the year, and it is given high ratings for its tenderness and flavor.

When my friend Gerry Warren of Slow Food Seattle organized a tasting of prime cuts of Churro lamb that had been slaughtered at twelve, eighteen, and twenty-four months of age, the results surprised him. The twelve-month-old lamb was rated "outstanding" or "as good as it gets."

But unlike the meat of other sheep breeds, Churros seldom take on the stronger, *muttony* flavor that many novices find to be disagreeable. The eighteen- and twenty-four-month-old prime cuts were still found to be enjoyable, especially if braised.

In fact, Gerry may be understating the superiority of Churro lamb. By 2017, a bone-in, five-pound Navajo-Churro leg of lamb could be retailed for $105 from Heritage Foods USA, or $17 to $21 a pound. Few other breeds of sheep can garner such prices.

Churro wool also has many unique attributes that the best weavers know how to highlight. Churros are double-coated, with a long-stapled, coarser outer carpet wool that makes up a fifth of the weight of an average fleece.

The finer, glossier undercoat is shorter stapled, less greasy, and prone to holding onto burs and composes the other four-fifths. The wool comes in fourteen color patterns, ranging from charcoal black, to blue, to dark brown, to gray/tan.

Fortunately, people are beginning to realize the value of Churro fleeces and they now garner respectable prices at festivals and over the internet.

Diné artists' weavings made from 100 percent Churro wool sell for thousands of dollars and receive national awards at Wool Festivals. The wool from the double-fleeced Churros may sell for thirty times what it did during the worst years, so producers now have two good sources of income from the same animal.

But higher prices are not the only reason Diné families want to keep Navajo-Churro. Whenever my wife and I get to attend the Sheep Is Life festival, held at Diné College each summer, we are touched by the abundant traditional knowledge still being passed on from generation to generation of herders and weavers.

As Roy Kady—director for the Navajo Lifeway project that maintains such lore—once put it, "We're responsible for the breed. This animal that is so sacred to us, we are nonexistent without them. In any means that we can preserve them, we're open to that."

I once hosted Roy Kady and two other singers of traditional sheep songs at the Museum of Northern Arizona for what may have been the first-ever formal "Sheep Boy" concert in the US. As Roy told stories between singing beautiful songs in the Diné language, I began to understand that his efforts are about far more than the sheep themselves. He was maintaining a lifeway that might otherwise disappear from the face of the earth.

That's exactly why a number of Diné herders flew to Spain to participate in a Global Gathering of Nomadic and Transhumant Pastoralists hosted by Via Campesina. They are part of a global movement not only to save rare breeds but to maintain traditional corridors for herders who move many kinds of flocks from mountain pastures in the summer to lower, more protected valleys for the winter.

And so, within the last decade, collaborative conservation has developed an entirely fresh expression: the collective efforts of herders of sheep, goats, camels, yaks, llamas, vicunas, and reindeer from all around the world. These efforts have culminated in the 2010 Mera Declaration of the Global Gathering of Women Pastoralists, which, among other issues, asked that all governments do the following:

1. Recognize the essential role of pastoralists in global environmental sustainability, including the conservation of biodiversity, mitigation of climate change, and combating desertification.
2. Ensure the equal rights of pastoralist women and recognize their key roles in society. This includes the recognition of the work of women pastoralists as a valid profession and as a fundamental component of pastoralism.
3. Recognize pastoralist mobility as a fundamental right.
4. Ensure and defend pastoral access to resources, including our traditional grazing lands.

For me, at least, it is hard to imagine Navajo-Churro sheep continuing to survive without American consumers starting to care more about grass-fed or pasture-raised meat. The flavor and texture of Navajo-Churro lamb come not just from its unique genetics but from the way the breed forages for its food, roaming the sagebrush-dominated steppes and the pinyon-juniper woodlands of the semiarid Southwest.

Churros are not really grazers of grass as much as they are browsers of a set of shrubs and herbs that most of us know merely as desert wildflowers. We jokingly say that Churro lamb should be marketed as "sage-fed" rather than "grass-fed," since most Navajo families I know never spice their meat with culinary herbs because the fragrance of sagebrush is already so deeply embedded in the lamb.

The capacity of sheep and lambs to take on a distinctive and deeply memorable terroir may be one reason *grass-fed* (read *sage-fed*, etc.) production is growing more rapidly for sheep in Western states than for beef, bison, or goat. From 2012 to 2017, the number of grass-fed lamb producers in the twelve westernmost states of the lower forty-eight has risen from 54 to 141, 2.6 times the earlier number. Grass-fed beef producers have increased only 2.1 times the earlier number and goats 1.3 times the former count.

Something special is happening with the production of grass-fed lamb, especially Navajo-Churro lamb, that bears further investigation. Whatever it is, it delights me as much as I'm delighted by the way Diné and Hispanic herders originally came together to save the breed. My pleasure may be surpassed only by that of the Diné herders themselves, who now share stories of their successes with other herders from thirty-two different countries all around the world.

CHAPTER 10

Immigrant Grains

Hᴀᴠᴇ ʏᴏᴜ ᴇᴠᴇʀ ɢᴏᴛᴛᴇɴ ᴛᴏ ᴛʜᴇ ʙᴏᴛᴛᴏᴍ of a cooking pot full of rice, wheat berry pilaf, or pearl couscous and scooped up the last, slightly charred morsels of those cereal grains? Did they have a sweet, nutty flavor, reminiscent of roasted pinyons or toasted hazelnuts? Did they stick to your stomach, filling you with the satisfaction of being truly nourished?

That's how I feel each time I finish off the last remnants of a dish of Carolina Gold rice from Anson Mills in South Carolina, heirloom buckwheat from Shagbark Seed and Mill in Ohio, or White Sonora white berries from Hayden Flour Mills in Arizona. They give me the sensation that grains are not just commodities or "staples" but delicacies so flavorful that I'd rather have them than some fluffy, sugar-laden dessert.

I must admit that what I cherish about each of these grains is not merely its flavor or texture. It is the larger satisfaction of seeing entire supply chains of heritage grains restored before my very eyes.

Moreover, these supply chains are being restored by friends who are among the finest mentors and most generous collaborators with whom I have ever been blessed to work. They have revived grains that had become economically inviable and functionally obsolete in our cuisine.

Somehow—in a matter of just a few years—these innovators have halted the extinction of historically significant cereals. But they have also created niche markets for reviving entire regional cuisines, benefiting not only farmers and eaters but every other human link in the food supply chain.

As for the revival of Carolina Gold rice—an African grain thought to be introduced to Charleston as early as 1686—I am speaking of networks of collaboration formed by Glenn Roberts, CEO of Anson Mills and David Shields, chairman of the Carolina Gold Rice Foundation.

David remembers his first real encounter with Glenn in 2003, when they were both at a conference in Charleston that was exploring traditional cuisines of the Caribbean and the adjacent coastal Southeastern US. The Anson Mills founder proposed the following outrageous notion: "I want to bring back Carolina Gold rice. I want there to be authentic Lowcountry cuisine again. Not the local branch of southern cooking incorporated."

According to David, after Glenn got off the stage, he came up to David, whom he hardly knew at that time, and asked him an impertinent question that has bonded them together for the last two decades: "He asked me, point-blank, whether I wished to participate in the effort to restore authentic Lowcountry cuisine . . . [Until then,] I had always pegged him as a preservationist rather than a restorationist."

But no more. David jumped on the wagon with Glenn and went careening through the Low Country, seeking out one rare foodstuff or cooking technique after another. They were looking for ways to echo but not dogmatically replicate the Carolina culinary traditions of the previous three centuries.

Along with David and Glenn's work to revitalize a Lowcountry cuisine, I also value the efforts of other unforgettable characters in the Low Country. A few immediately come to mind: they include Rollen Chalmers, an African American cultivator of the rice who lives and farms in Oakatie, South Carolina, and Ira Wallace, co-owner of the Southern

Exposure Seed Exchange, who distributes seeds of this rice for planting. Ira also markets seven hundred other heirloom seed varieties as well. This kind of work takes a foodshed of willing, risk-taking players from many backgrounds and skill sets.

All of these entrepreneurs have helped revitalize the heritage grains and legumes that have long been associated with place-based cuisines. But none of this work would have happened without Glenn's highly effective, if peculiar, methods. He has the charisma to engage people from many walks of life and the wisdom to bring them together to restore something bigger and more delicious than anything any individual person could single-handedly create.

When Glenn Roberts and David Shields speak of reviving an entire traditional cuisine, they are not only talking about growing particular food crops. They are also exploring how these heirloom varieties can be intercropped and rotated in a farming system; how they can be milled, stored, transported, and cooked in ways that create new local livelihoods; and how to foster the mutually beneficial interactions among farmers, millers, chefs, and bakers that anchor all this work.

You may presume that I am giving a bit too much credit to these innovators, given that you yourself have tasted breads or soups or beers made of other heritage grains: Turkey Hard Red wheat, Red Fife wheat, Roy's Calais flint corn, purple-hulled barley, grain amaranth, or huauzontle, a quinoa-like seed. But as artisanal baker Don Guerra once aptly explained to me, such work is not about the bread alone nor merely about saving old-timey seeds.

The easiest way for me to describe the difference is by telling you about my own futile efforts in the eighties and nineties to get anyone at all interested in White Sonora wheat. That was before the genius of what Glenn and David were doing began to sink into my hard head.

During December 1975, I was with my friend Tom Sheridan when we were given a few viable kernels of "Sonora Blanca," a soft white-bread wheat introduced from Spain, in the Rio San Miguel and Rio Sonora watersheds, not even one hundred miles south of the US-Mexico border. It was while we were doing other work on the ethnobotany of that desert region. We had been keeping our ears and eyes open for any notice of ancient grains and legumes, for we had already come upon remnants of *maiz reventador*, the oldest surviving popcorn of North America.

Those grains of Sonora Blanca gifted to us looked much like what the first Jesuit missionaries to the Americas called a *candeal* wheat, one of the types of grain that was permissible to use in making communion wafers. We now know that the descendants of *candeal* wheat have become the oldest surviving landrace of wheat in North America, but when I first set my eyes upon its pale, oblong grains, it was already becoming rare.

The mestizo farmers whom Tom and I met had all grown up on White Sonora wheat and reventador corn but noted that they had become endangered ever since Green Revolution hybrid varieties had been introduced in the previous decade. In just a quarter century—from 1965 to 1990—White Sonora was rapidly replaced by another bread wheat with a similar name, Sonora 64. This new "Sonora" had been promoted as a "silver bullet" all across northern Mexico by Nobel Prize–winning geneticist Norman Borlaug, who worked out of a crop-breeding station two hundred miles farther south in Sonora.

The trouble was that, while Sonora 64 outproduced Sonora Blanca under irrigation, the new hybrid did not have the texture or taste of the heritage variety. The shift made Sonoran tortilla makers irate, for they felt that a higher yield of an inferior product was not a very good deal. They told their husbands to get rid of the hybrid and give them back Sonora Blanca, which they also called Flor de America.

But the millers working at larger diesel- and electric-powered mills in the region wanted only wanted Sonora 64. It was a homogeneous product that could be sold in the urban marketplace. The smaller, water-powered mills of the region were already in decline due to drought, and so the local milling of a diverse set of grains was becoming a thing of the past.

Finding themselves between a rock and a hard place, some women in Sonora held onto their own mule-turned grindstones called *tahonas* so that they could continue to grind their own tortilla flour rather than getting the poorer-quality mixed kinds from bigger flour mills in their region.

A few years later, I accidentally encountered this same heritage wheat in the US while riding through the desert in Arizona with my teacher and ethnobiology pioneer Amadeo Rea. He took a winding dirt road back to a small homestead of a Native American couple, David and Rosie, who had been friends of his for years. At that time, their residence was by the edge of a small grain field along the Santa Cruz River, but they had earlier labored as farmworkers among other tribes and among Anglo and Hispanic farmers as well.

David had grown White Sonora off and on for many years. We talked for a while about the old harvesting and milling traditions. They used to harvest their wheat by hand with sickles and then thresh it with horses running in a circle around a special floor called an *era* in Spanish.

Rosie showed us how to put red-hot coals in a basket filled with wheat kernels and shake it in a way that roasted the kernels, which were then ground into a fine powdery *pinole* flour. It was delicious alone as a trail food or mixed with a little hot water or milk.

Not long after that, Amadeo called me up and asked me to go back with him to see Rosie. David had passed away, and Rosie was trying to decide what to do with all of his seeds and farm implements. She felt she was too old to maintain their farm work on her own.

"Can you make sure someone will grow it?" Rosie asked Amadeo. "I don't want it to die, so I've decided not to grind all of it into flour. But I don't have anyone with me here who can grow it any longer."

Amadeo assured her that we would try to find someone who could grow it out, since he and I knew Indian and Mexican farmers on both sides of the border who kept different seeds at their homes.

By that time, while learning to plow fields using draft horses, I had helped hand-sow wheat in fields both north and south of the Arizona-Sonora border: some Pima Club, some Early Baart, and some White Sonora wheat. I had never kept wheat seed nor grown sizeable quantities of White Sonora myself but just held on to those first few kernels from the Rio San Miguel.

Rosie suddenly gave Amadeo a Folger's coffee can full of White Sonora wheat seed from David's last harvest, in hope that the variety would not be lost.

Amadeo parsed the seed she gave him out to various friends who grew it in small plots over the next few years at their own homes. Just enough was grown to replenish the seed stock, but it was hardly ever enough to make much bread or tortillas.

Besides, the heirloom seed movement at that time—in the early eighties—was about backyard gardeners growing vegetables and beans, not grains. Very few farmers with sizeable plots of land were then engaged with these grains, and very few home cooks (let alone chefs) were trying out a wide range of whole grain varieties.

And so the wheat sat there—on a shelf in a shed or in a major jar in a refrigerator—for years, without anyone showing much interest in it. A few years passed before I met Thom Leonard—the first heritage grain grower and baker I ever knew.

When I first encountered Thom, he had already learned artisanal baking from a European immigrant but was working as a journalist for *East/West* magazine covering food and agriculture. Then he jumped to the Land Institute in Salina, Kansas, where he gained a keen sense of how to collect, grow, and evaluate heritage grains. The next stage in his metamorphosis was running his own heritage grain bakery in Lawrence, Kansas, followed by another in Athens, Georgia. I did not know it until many years later, but he also trained my friend Don Guerra in how to bake slow-fermented dough from heritage grains into fantastically flavored and textured breads.

We began to hear that innovators like Sally Fox in California, Glenn Roberts in South Carolina, and Will Bonsall and Eli Shiva Rogosa in Maine were ramping up interest in heritage grains among artisanal bakers on both coasts. The Zimmermans had just begun a milling operation in the back room of a restaurant in Phoenix, but we were still waiting for enough bakers and brewers in our own region to get interested. With the local food movement taking off, we had little trouble getting people excited about heirloom vegetables, beans, fruits, and nuts, but for many reasons, the revival of heritage grains lagged far behind.

Then I met Glenn Roberts, who was willing to gift our community six tons of White Sonora wheat. Glenn and I had been traveling together to a heritage grain producers meeting when we first brainstormed about how his strategies for bringing back Carolina Gold rice might be tried with White Sonora wheat.

Glenn was not just the CEO of Anson Mills; he had a deeper knowledge of grain supply chains than anyone I had ever met. His mother had mastered the Afro-American tradition of the Geechee or Gullah black skillet cooking of the Sea Islands, so he got an early taste of the Carolina rice kitchen.

As a young man, Glenn had also labored as a harvester in Low Country agricultural fields, as an oysterman on fishing boats, and as a cook in the restaurants of Charleston. He had also worked as a restaurant designer and commercial pilot before coming back to Low Country to open Anson Mills in a small warehouse and office complex off the beaten track in Columbia, South Carolina.

In short, he had personally worked in just about every link of the food chain and could see how they all functioned together.

Glenn and David Shields's work in the Low Country showed me new possibilities—the restoration of a dynamic food supply chain from farmer to baker, brewer, chef, and eater. As Glenn explained to me, he began harvesting Carolina Gold in fields south of Charleston in 1998. His neighbor Richard Schulze repatriated the grain from a historic collection of *Oryza glaberrima*, an upland rice species distinct from the one that dominated most gene banks that rice breeders used.

Glenn then worked tirelessly to expand the grower's network to include farms and plantations in Georgia, North Carolina, Texas, and Virginia so that all his proverbial eggs would not be in one basket should a hurricane or drought devastate a large swath of Low Country.

But Glenn did not merely want to buy from conventional growers and pay the asking prices for their products. Through the Carolina Gold Rice Foundation, he, David Shields, and Richard Schulze supported sustainable farmers like Rollen Chalmers in every way imaginable—from giving them tons of "starter" seed, to offering technical advice about how to become certified as organic, to loaning them specialized equipment.

If they were willing to organically grow multiple crops associated with the Carolina rice kitchen traditions, all the better. Once they achieved their first ample harvests, the farmers were then encouraged to donate quality seed back to the foundation so that it could be tithed to others who wished to grow Low Country staples like Carolina Gold rice, flint corns, crowder peas, or benne sesame seeds.

Rollen Chalmers, who grows thirty acres of Carolina Gold and Charleston rice just ten minutes from downtown Savannah, Georgia, has also experimented with growing Sea Island cotton and indigo on behalf of a Geechee community heritage museum out on Daufuskie Island.

While his own family and his in-laws grew the rice when he was a child, it was the collaboration with his colleagues in the Carolina Gold Rice Foundation that brought these other Low Country seeds back into his hands. Rollen explained, "My grandfather grew his Gold rice for survival, my family depended on it. But I also developed a great relationship with these gentlemen [from the foundation], and I'm grateful for the knowledge and support they've shared with me."

At the same time, Glenn was also working with innovative chefs like Sean Brock to integrate these grains and legumes into gruels, gumbos, and Hoppin' Johns characteristic of the Low Country traditions. Sean has gone so far as to take the sous chefs from his Husk restaurant in historic Charleston back to West Africa, where both the seeds and the culinary techniques appear to have originated.

By interacting with African chefs and home cooks there, they have gained extraordinary insights about how to bring out the unique qualities of these ingredients.

For Sean Brock, it is about both the backstory and the quality of the ingredients. The Charleston chef has called Carolina Gold rice "the most flavorful rice I have ever tasted."

And now an African American ethnobotanist from Trinidad—Francis Morean—is collaborating with Gullah/Geechee chief Benjamin J. Dennis to explore the remarkable links between the cultures and rice cuisines of West Africa, the Merikan settlements in the Palo Seco area on the Caribbean island of Trinidad, and Gullah of the Sea Islands in the Southeast US. As Chief B. J. Dennis told Francis Morean, "It is up to us to tell our own story [connected to the historic travels of the gold rice] correctly. And it makes my heart happy, chasing my ancestral roots through food."

These cross-cultural exchanges may play a small role in healing historic wounds created by the African and Caribbean slave trade to the US, where African Americans long suffered on the Southeast's rice plantations.

Carolina Gold rice and other Anson Mills heirlooms are now sent to and served in hundreds of restaurants across the nation, although Low Country chefs are their most ardent devotees. Glenn wanted to help us accomplish something similar with White Sonora wheat. That's why

Glenn shipped us the six tons of seed of a White Sonora strain collected in Durango, Mexico—one that the Carolina Gold Rice Foundation had obtained from a growing program they organized with California heirloom crop enthusiasts Sally Fox and Monica Spiller.

With additional support from a USDA SARE grant, we began our fledgling supply chain at one of the first places that this grain grew in the United States, the San Ignacio de Túbac Presidio, established in what is now Southern Arizona in 1752.

Don Guerra, the artisanal baker, was there, offering a dozen different loaves of bread made with White Sonora wheat. Jeff and Emma Zimmerman of Hayden Flour Mills were there to anchor the entire supply chain by purchasing their harvest for fair prices. Chris Schmidt and other Native Seeds/SEARCH staff were there as comanagers of this sustainable agriculture promotion grant. Steve Sossaman was one of several farmers who participated, and he later offered Hayden Flour Mills a larger space for its initial operations.

But there were also Hispanic food folklorists from the Southwest Folkways Alliance; small business promoters from Local Forest Arizona; growers from Forever Yong Farm, Avalon Gardens, and the Canelo Project; brewers and caterers; market managers; and journalists. And we passed on word of our discussions to Ramona and Terry Button, who soon began to grown White Sonora for the Gila River Indian Community, and to Cornelio Molina Valencia, who wished to reintroduce it to the Yaqui Indian community in Sonora, Mexico.

We were immediately interested in assuring that the growers' network included other native farmers from the San Xavier O'odham and Gila River Indian communities in Arizona, as well as the Rio Sonora and Yaqui communities in Sonora. These exchanges not only have panned out but have grown the White Sonora value chain. They helped diversify the products made from this wheat as well as the recipients who bought and ate them.

There are now three mills in Arizona, and Barrio Grains Co-op is in its first stages of production and distribution. In Mexico, a heritage grain production initiative in the Yaqui community of Sonora started by Cornelio is into its third year of producing White Sonora wheat. There are also discussions that have begun about restoring the historic grain mills in other watersheds of Sonora.

More than 150 acres of White Sonora are currently grown in Arizona alone. For the first time in a half century, White Sonora products are now available every day of the week in farmers' markets, gift shops, groceries, breweries, bakeries, and community-supported agriculture projects.

Our region's heritage grain supply chain is now in better shape than it has been for more than sixty years, when the drought of the fifties forced dryland farmers to abandon their rain-fed fields and mills closed because there was no waterpower to turn their grindstones.

Thanks to Hayden Flour Mills, the supply chain for one grain—White Sonora wheat—has helped bring back at least a dozen heirloom cereals and legumes. We now have a full-fledged regional *foodweb*, involving many players from diverse cultures—Hispanic, Yaqui, O'odham, Chinese, and Anglo.

It is a revival that would have been unimaginable even twenty years ago. And it has created dozens of new jobs in four counties in the borderlands at a time when those jobs are desperately needed.

White Sonora wheat might be the gateway grain of the Sonoran Desert foodshed, but you can't have a regional cuisine that is revived by bread or tortillas alone. The resurgence of tepary beans, mottled lima beans, chickpeas, barley, cushaw squash, wild oregano, and chiltepins are just as essential. White Sonoran wheat berries were often used with tepary beans, chiltepins, and oreganos in posoles quite different in taste and texture than the corn posoles of northern New Mexico. And yet the size of the market for the wheat variety itself remains much smaller than that for the beans and spices.

One problem is that it remains a lot cheaper to produce and process commodity grains than heritage varieties. The commodified cereals remain so easy to grow, mill, store, ship, and subsidize on a large scale that the price per pound of their flour is affordable to nearly any consumer, rich or poor. Yet, they lack flavor and texture.

And so, there are a handful of heritage grains and legumes that are making local comebacks—from Pinquito beans in California to Bloody Butcher and Hickory King dent corns in Appalachia. Unfortunately, these are exceptions that prove the rule . . . at least for now.

A whole host of other grains and beans are in precipitous decline—including American hog peanuts, Indian ricegrass, little-leaf barley, jackbeans, Sonoran panicgrass, the American groundnut, Price's groundnut, the potato beans, Palmer's saltgrass, huauzontle, Job's tears, and peavines. Some, like the Price's groundnut, are federally listed as threatened or endangered.

In his book *Southern Provisions*, David Shields explains why Glenn Roberts has succeeded on a scale that has evaded other regional efforts:

"Roberts was a pragmatist. He realized that to make an effective intervention in America's food supply system, he had to avoid direct competition with the industrial food production and seed production companies. He had to scale his operation to the demands of that sector of the restaurant world fixed on superlative ingredient quality. He had to price his products to cover costs (an issue, since landrace cultivars tend to be less productive), and grow them with such care that their quality fully warranted their higher price . . . He located what was rare . . . and grew it so as to maximize its innate flavor . . . Once he established his business, he expanded cultivars, growers, fields, rotations."

In fact, when some so-called heritage grains are commoditized, their taste, texture, nutritional value, and backstory suffer. This has been the case with the so-called wild rice produced by California paddy growers and the blue corn, originally from New Mexico Pueblos, now grown by Texas Panhandle farmers.

The cultural ties that first prompted us to call these grains "heritage" or "heirloom" begin to unravel, appropriated by an industry that fails to recognize or benefit their original stewards. Sooner or later, growing these grains ceases to be about biological conservation, cultural restoration, or for that matter, taste.

But when small-scale and culturally responsible efforts gain traction, they produce more than food or income. They remind us where we *and* the grain came from, what has nourished us, and that such connections are worth caring for. In communities with histories of racial and class conflict, heritage foods can bring diverse peoples together around a common table for healing and celebration.

The point is not lost on me that White Sonora wheat was first introduced to our region in 1630 by Jesuit priests who wanted to convert the locals with a communion wafer and wine. But today, collective efforts to restore this grain are uniting people of many faiths, cultures, and political persuasions. In ways old and new, religious and secular, we are now seeing White Sonora's historic role in our communities shift from one begun by colonization and conversion toward one that is far closer to true multicultural communion.

CHAPTER 11

Urban Growers and Rare Fruits

Have you bit into an heirloom apple so crisp and bracing, so fresh and tart, that it puts Granny Smith to shame? Have you ever slipped a date across your lips that is so sweet and buttery that it melts in your mouth and leaves you weak in the knees?

That's exactly what rare fruits like the Green Newtown Pippin can do—and what the dozen apple cultivars that dominate our grocery stores can never touch. That's what a highly perishable Black Sphinx date can do—and what the fossilized, cardboard-textured dried dates shipped halfway around the world can never equal.

You have to wonder, Why do most Americans purchase just a few kinds of mediocre fruits and nuts when eight thousand varieties of at least fifty other species are readily available in our nurseries, farmers' markets, and backyards?

And why have we let another ten thousand perfectly edible fruit and nut heirlooms die out in our orchards, fall off of our tables, and evaporate from our mugs and wineglasses?

I guess I take this impoverishment of taste personally because my grandpa—"Papa John" Ferhat Nabhan, a Syrian immigrant and fruit peddler—began to discuss this dilemma with me when I was barely five years of age. He would come to our house after hours of driving his fruit peddler's truck from neighborhood to neighborhood in the Indian Dunes, lamenting a fact that, by 1957, seemed painfully obvious to him: *Most midwesterners hardly knew what good fruit tasted like anymore.* They would complain about the pomes and berry clusters that were soft or slightly bruised but blushing with ripeness and fragrant in the readiness to be eaten. They would let the best fruits hang too long on the tree or sit in a bowl until they would spoil.

He would speak to me about such things as if I were his confidante, confessor, or business partner . . . and sometimes all three at once: "Gary Baul, now you tell me, habibi, why do these Amirkhani don't want to eat fruit while it's ribe and tasty, but they waste their monies on the ones that are hard as wood or flavor like corn starch? Why do I still bring them so many kind of fruit when all they want is Mack-in-Tosh or Dead-de-Lishus? Here, I bring you the ones the rich beople don't want, the fig, the abricot, the Green Gage blum, the bom-a-granate. Here, habibi, let me blop it right in your mouth, so you can taste what they are missing!"

I don't believe that any of us who experienced such flavor and fragrance when we were children ever leave our love for that kind of sensuous pleasure behind us . . . It may go dormant for a while, but it never dies.

I suppose that's why I tend an orchard today with thirty-five species of heirloom fruits, nuts, berries, and perennial succulents and have planted more than 150 varieties of them since moving to our five acres in 2010.

As one of my cousins once kidded me, I had to get three college degrees and work another twenty years in agricultural and natural resource sciences before beginning to grow the very same fruits that our grandfather did—without a high school diploma.

Perhaps Papa John Nabhan was one of the few of his generation who recognized the homogenization of fruit production that occurred within his lifetime. During his decades peddling fruit in the Great Lakes region, he had close at hand no less than thirty-six varieties of apples, five cherries, twelve grapes, four peaches, eight pears, two persimmons, thirteen plums, and twenty-three berries that are now threatened or endangered *because they have fallen out of household and restaurant use.*

In central and southern Appalachia—the region that maintains the greatest diversity of heirloom and heritage fruits, nuts, and berries, with more than 630 distinct varieties in cultivation—at least sixty-four may have been lost in recent decades. And yet another 280 varieties, mostly apples, are now considered threatened or endangered due to their limited availability in nurseries, scion exchanges, and botanical gardens.

In California, at least eighty-eight fruit varieties that were once widely cultivated are now threatened or endangered. And this is despite the diligent work of members of the California Rare Fruit Growers such as Todd Kennedy, David Karp, John Valenzuela, and Amigo Bob Cantisano.

If you think this is just a farmer's choice issue, you might be surprised by the results of a survey of apple growers in Ohio. They, like many other farmers, want to grow a diversity of fruits but can't find enough willing takers.

As one of them once told me in the bluntest of terms, "If consumers aren't interested in all but three of four kinds of apples, sooner or later I'm going to have to cull the others from my orchard."

Unless something changes. And ironically, in a growing number of cities around the country, it is urban dwellers who are leading the change.

Let me take you to an unlikely setting for the restoration of rare fruits: Metro Phoenix, in the Southwest's Sunbelt, what one British writer has called the most unsustainable city on the face of the earth. And yet, as if to prove him wrong, a groundswell of local support in Metro Phoenix has kept alive one of the rarest and most delicious fruits in North America with virtually no federal, state, or philanthropic support.

The fruit in question is the Black Sphinx date, whose palm trees I had the pleasure of living under in the late 1980s in the Arcadia District, below Camelback Mountain. In fact, that Phoenix neighborhood may be one of the few residential areas in the country *designed* to produce fruit.

A dozen Black Sphinx date palms, as well as orange and grapefruit trees, surrounded our house on a half-acre lot in the midst of Metro Phoenix. Palm trees also grew in the twenty-three acres that composed our neighbors' yards.

As originally conceived by Arizona pioneer and philanthropist Ellen Amelia Goodbody Brophy, the Date and Citrus Homes Subdivision of the Phoenix Date Company was to cover forty-seven acres, with fifty-five palms per acre in neat rows that would shade all the houses from the scorching desert sun. Residents lived in the orchard and could pick all the citrus they wished, but the 250 to 350 pounds of dates per palm would be harvested by the company's crews.

Legend has it that a chance seedling of what we now call the Black Sphinx date was discovered under a mature date palm of the Hayani variety off Lafayette Avenue in the sleepy western town of Phoenix, Arizona, in 1925. Its twelve initial offshoots were propagated by root division and transplanted out to by a horticulturally curious Phoenician named Roy Franklin. Roy decided that the misfit should not be rogued out but protected until it came to maturity and produced a fruit, to see if keeping this "sport of a date" was worth it.

As soon as it fruited and its plump, tender dates were found to have the taste of honey, caramel, and vanilla in their melting flesh, Franklin sought out Ellen Brophy to help save and promote this unique date palm. She became its guardian and champion.

After Ellen Brophy's untimely death in 1934, her son Frank assumed the task of making sure his mother's dream bore fruit on the six hundred palms she had left in her wake. It was Frank who named the new variety Black Sphinx, and he carefully described its rare qualities for an Arizona Agricultural Experiment Station Bulletin. Renaming their plantation the Sphinx Date Company, Frank expanded Black Sphinx palm plantings to six thousand acres in the Valley of the Sun, producing as much as one hundred thousand pounds of dates in the best of years.

I believe I met Frank Brophy only once, just a couple years before he died, but two of his descendants are among my neighbors in the Sonoita Plains of Southeastern Arizona. I have even done a bit of field research on yuccas and agaves on their historic Spanish land grant, the San Ignacio del Babocamori Ranch, established in 1832.

Most of the Black Sphinx palms were planted from slow-growing offshoots onto a square mile of irrigated land just south of the iconic Camelback Peak. Each was originally tended, harvested, and sorted in a packing shed managed by the Phoenix Date Co. and sold at a gift shop at the same location.

They were soon in demand as the premier fresh date across the entire US, but they were so delicate and prone to ferment that most of their devotees would come to Arizona with the expressed purpose of experiencing this manna in late fall.

Frank Brophy was not merely blowing his own family's horn when he wrote that the Black Sphinx was "far and away the best date grown in the world." It was in demand by commercial date palm growers as far away as Australia, and he could charge $100 a palm seedling at a time when other varieties sold for only $5 to $10 a tree.

In 1947, he registered it as a unique variety with the American Society for Horticultural Science, comparing it favorably to its probable ancestors, the Hayani, Bahri, and Khadrawi dates imported from Egypt.

A half century after Ellen Goodbody Brophy died, my family moved into a home in the last twenty acres of the plantation that held 98 percent of all the Black Sphinx dates in the world. The land values were so high around Camelback Mountain that we could only rent there, for the likes of Alice Cooper, Barry Goldwater, and Joe Garagiola were living nearby.

Most of the palms on the edges of the Arcadia District had already been bulldozed to make room for trophy homes. The packing shed and gift shop had been moved away from the neighborhood, and there was only one man in Metro Phoenix who cared enough about the dates to regularly organize palm-climbing crews to pollinate and harvest them.

The man's name was Harry Polkow, a.k.a. Harry Polk, a scholar of philosophy who had helped initiate the Gentle Strength Food Co-op while still a student at Arizona State University.

Harry would come around to our home and others to alert us that a crew of palm trimmers, pollinators, and harvesters born in the tropics of Mexico would be coming into our yard in the following weeks to do their work and share whatever portion of the harvest with us we cared to keep.

Being at least a decade younger than Harry, I looked up to him as a role model . . . especially when he wrapped a belt around himself and a palm trunk and scaled up the tree to pollinate its flowers. He combined lofty thinking with pragmatism in a manner I had never seen in anyone else. He single-handedly kept Black Sphinx dates in the marketplace for another two decades after the Brophys had phased out their special relationships with these date palms.

And while most of our neighbors were only vaguely aware that they were living in the shadows of one of America's most delicious rare fruits, a few of us in Harry's circle realized they had been praised by the likes of the Eisenhauers, Kennedys, Rockefellers, Johnsons, Goldwaters, and Bushes, as well as Lilian Hellman, Gene Autry, Lilian Gish, Bing Crosby, and Chef Alice Waters.

When Harry Polk finally threw in the towel, the Phoenix community initially feared that no one else with comparable passion and skill would maintain the harvest.

Ultimately, others did in fact step up to the plate, and the 350 remaining palms in the Arcadia District have found new harvesters and champions. At least two dozen Black Sphinx palms also persist in other locales, but all are suffering because of seasonal changes triggered by climate change or the effects of heat islands.

And yet the draw to the temporal pleasures of eating Black Sphinx dates remains strong among Phoenicians. When the local power company offered to pay Arcadia District residents $100 per tree to remove and destroy Black Sphinx palms that were encroaching on their power line rights-of-way, a fierce protest erupted.

The power company relented and now offers residents with palms near electric lines $1,000 per tree if it is allowed to carefully move them to places in their yards were the palms can grow without interference!

The Phoenix Zoo and the Arizona State University Arboretum are working to devise best practices in propagation and transplant while this genetic stock is now conserved for the long haul in a USDA Repository in Thermal, California, and at the Yuma Mesa Agricultural Center in Somerton, Arizona.

Now heralded as "the Mysterious Date Palms of Phoenix," the trees and their fruit have quite a reputation. Hardly a year goes by without some journalist doing a story about the historic, culinary, and community-building value of Black Sphinx dates. They are now boarded onto the Slow Food Biodiversity Foundation's International Ark of Taste.

For more than a decade, I have been an avid fan of other urban fruit tree restoration projects around the country: Guerilla Grafters in the San Francisco Bay area of California; the Chicago Rarities Orchard Project in Illinois; the Portland Fruit Tree Project in Oregon; and RELEAF, with its affiliates, Trees for Tucson and Mission Gardens in Arizona.

But if there is one project that stands out above all others, it is the Green Newtown Pippin Restoration and Celebration project. It has forged partnerships among groups as diverse as the New York Restoration Project, Green Apple Gleaners, Slow Food NYC Harvest Time program, the Children's Magic Garden, the Earth School, the Metropolitan Waterfront Alliance, the Juan Morel Campos School, Green Drinks NYC, the Greenbelt Native Plants Center, and other community organizations in all parts of the city.

The initiative has been spearheaded by an effusive community activist and writer named Erik Baard, who clearly loves this apple like no other.

I myself may be partial to this recovery effort for a personal reason: many of my own family of Syrian immigrants first settled in the South Ferry neighborhood of Brooklyn after a few months in the Battery Park tenements called "Little Syria" in Manhattan.

At that time, about a century ago, many row houses had at least one Green Newtown Pippin tree in their postage-stamp-sized yards. Its sprightly, crisp, juicy, aromatic fruit was the pride of New York back then and in nearly all of Brooklyn's homemade ciders, both hard and sweet.

Sometime between 1720 and 1750, the original Newtown Pippin tree gained recognition on Long Island, probably on the estate of Greshom Moore in the settlement of Newtown. That neighborhood in Queens is now called Elmhurst, and Gershom's estate stood almost exactly where Broadway crosses Forty-Fifth Street.

By 1805, scion wood cuttings of this green-tinged, finely textured apple were in such demand by orchardists in New York and New England that the original tree died from exhaustion and wounds from being constantly pruned. Orchardists paid this death little matter, since the variety was everywhere and with everyone by then.

As Rowan Jacobsen has quipped, "Like Forrest Gump, the Newtown Pippin has managed to intersect with an improbable number of historic personages and places over the course of its career and has shown a knack for effortless success at whatever it was called to do."

Those not-too-shabby historic personages include the likes of Benjamin Franklin, George Washington, Thomas Jefferson, James Madison, and Queen Victoria. Queen Victoria so favored Green Newtown Pippins over other apples that she encouraged the British Parliament to lift the import duty on them, opening up the flow of tons of these apples to the British Isles up until World War I.

After the war, the renewal of import duty quashed the commercial value of Newtown Pippins, and production declined.

While the apples continued to be grown commercially in some orchards in Upstate New York, the only company that still took a sizeable share of the Newtown Pippin harvest was Martinelli's. If you've sipped Martinelli's Gold Medal sparkling cider, you've tasted a blend of juices from Newtowns and five other classic American apples.

Enter Erik Baard, the Queens native who first heard stories of this legendary fruit in 2005 while investigating how its historic nursery grounds—Newtown Creek in Elmhurst—had become so toxic that the US Environmental Protection Agency had declared it a Superfund site.

Baard was determined to restore these barren "brown fields" back to greenery, fertility, fecundity, and health.

"How had we as a city forgotten about this beautiful legacy?" Erik asked. He suggested planting a "Founding Fathers Grove" of Green Newtown Pippin apple trees right at the mouth of Newtown Creek. While his initial modest proposal became hopelessly bogged down by bureaucracy and was soon put on hold, Erik Baard's vision bloomed into something far larger.

Why not plant Green Newtown Pippins in iconic landscapes in all five New York boroughs—Queens, Harlem, the Bronx, Manhattan, and Brooklyn—and reaffirm its place as *the* legendary apple of the Big Apple?

After getting planting stock discounted or donated by several sources, including Cummins Nursery and the USDA Plant Introduction Station in Geneva, Baard somehow multiplied his resources with in-kind gifts from dozens of other willing players. By the end of 2011, the alliance had planted more than one thousand Green Newtown Pippin apple trees at more than fifty sites in Metro New York.

The alliance declared 2012 to be the Interfaith Year for the Newtown Pippin Restoration and Celebration, bringing the Jamaica Masjid Al-Mamur (Jamaica Mosque), St. John the Divine Cathedral, the First Presbyterian Church of Newtown, and Old St. Patrick's Cathedral into the cadre of "heirloom apple sanctuary sites" within the city.

The plantings themselves have generated other political, cultural, and culinary initiatives. Councilman James Gennaro drafted a resolution that would designate the Newtown Pippin as New York City's official apple. A Pippin tree was ceremoniously planted in the rooftop garden above the Arsenal headquarters of NYC Parks and Recreation in Central Park.

Gift boxes of the Newtown Pippins were donated by Green Apple leaders to forty cultural leaders in the city. Tastings were held in the city's Office of Long-Term Planning and Sustainability.

And finally, Original Sin Hard Cider released the first new American "single heirloom varietal cider" from juices fresh-pressed exclusively from Newtown Pippins from its Broadway cidery in the heart of New York City.

By the way, it's gluten-free. The cider. Not the city.

Whether it is Erik Baard and his Pippinists restoring Newtown Pippin's rightful place in New York City or Tara Hui and her Guerilla Grafter commandos grafting twenty-four thousand fruit trees around San Francisco Bay, there is something going on in dozens of North American cities that bears watching even as it begins to bear fruit.

Hundreds of thousands of fruit- and nut-bearing trees—many of them heirlooms that were in historic decline—have recently been either newly planted or top-worked onto existing trees with scion wood from additional varieties through community-based efforts. Such grassroots efforts are surging in no fewer than twenty-five metro areas in Canada and the US, probably more.

Urban dwellers, both infants and elders, peoples of all colors and faiths, speakers of dozens of languages, have entered into a covenant to make this world a more delicious and sheltering place.

By planting trees, they are reducing the effects of urban heat islands in their cities, storing carbon in the ground, and increasing local food security, especially for the homeless and homesick who eat whatever they can find in parks, schoolyards, church gardens, and greenbelts.

If he had lived long enough to witness these efforts in places like his own adopted cityscape of Gary, Indiana, I'm sure that this restoration of America's fruitfulness would have made Papa John Nabhan proud. I can guess what he would say: *"Habibi, that's what Amirka is about: a place where all kinds can fruit."*

CHAPTER 12

Return of the Pollinators

Have you ever watched a hummingbird in midflight, the energy vibrating through its beating wings? Have you stood in awe at dusk as bats flew out of a cave and blanketed the evening sky?

Have you heard the buzz of honeybees or blue orchard bees as they wander flower to flower through an apple orchard? And have you tasted those apples, swelling with the pollination of the bees?

More than twenty years ago, as cofounder and director of the Forgotten Pollinators Campaign, I had the chance to do field research that allowed me to get to know these animal pollinators and many more intimately. They were some of the most ecstatic moments of sheer beauty that I've ever experienced during my forty years as a field biologist.

But pollinators are not just beautiful; they are critical to our food supply. In the 1990s, when my colleague Steve Buchmann and I first told people that one in every three bites we eat was brought to us by a pollinator, it was astonishing news to most of them.

Fortunately, the majority of Americans now realize that pollinators are worth a lot to our economy overall and to farmers' livelihoods in particular.

In fact, these services to just fifty-eight of the six hundred animal-pollinated crop species grown in North America are estimated to be worth more than $29 billion annually. That number alone should convince us that bees, birds, butterflies, and bats are worth conserving. Furthermore, it should bring home to us that their habitats are well worth restoring.

Nevertheless, what we claim to value isn't always reflected in our own patterns of consumption or in the way we treat the land. From the mid-1990s onward, I have visited many farms and ranches where the blossoms of crops were not pollinated in the summer simply because pollinators were scarce, which usually led to fruitless falls.

Worried by the steep declines in the populations of bees, butterflies, white-winged doves, and nectar-feeding bats, my Forgotten Pollinators Campaign codirectors, Stephen Buchmann and Mrill Ingram, and I began to speak out about the impending pollinator crisis in wild environments, traveling to more than two dozen states to deliver our dire message.

Later, when we realized that the loss of diverse pollinators was triggering reproductive failures of crops in our fields and orchards as well, we were among those who first warned of food-chain collapse.

In 1996, we called for a national policy on pollination in our book, *The Forgotten Pollinators*. And in 1998, twenty-one of us—beekeepers, botanists, conservation biologists, farmers, insect ecologists, nature writers, and zoologists—coauthored the first analysis of the pollinator crisis that attempted to shift national policies, published in the journal *Conservation Biology*.

These publications were cited more than eight hundred times in other publications, and, perhaps most importantly, they got very capable professionals in several government agencies involved. By 2007, the National Research Council and other US federal agencies had issued a major report on the crisis.

Policymakers were no longer just wringing their hands over the potential extinction of a single species. They had begun to consider *the extinction of ecological interactions*. While word on this issue had gotten out at last, we were not at all sure whether recognition of the problem would lead to any tangible actions to restore pollinator food chains to prevent their further collapse.

Then came the bad news. Ever more frequent spraying of herbicides—especially on corn and soybean crops engineered to withstand them—had dramatically reduced milkweed—by as much as 2.5 billion plants. And without milkweeds available as larval host plants (and their flowers as nectar sources), there can be no monarch butterflies because most of their caterpillars only forage on this genus of plants.

We were shocked to hear how sharply the number of monarchs migrating to Mexico was plummeting. Scientists reported a 95 percent decline in the size of the overwintering habitat occupied by the monarchs in the mountains of the Transvolcanic Belt in Mexico.

Soon similar news began to be reported from the Pacific coast, where the southernmost wintering sites near the US-Mexico border were being abandoned by monarchs altogether, while other sites were suffering steep declines.

By any standard, this was a staggering change in status for one of America's most iconic, beloved, and once ubiquitous creatures. The decline had been so rapid and so severe for the butterflies wintering both in Mexico and in coastal California that lepidopterist Robert Michael Pyle worried that the epic migration of monarchs itself was being endangered.

By spring 2015, when forty Americans were invited to Washington, DC, for the White House Pollinator Summit convened by President Obama, it was clear that pollinator declines were no longer just the concern of a few geeky scientists and fervent activists. That gathering was probably the first meeting ever held at the White House to propose "humanitarian" relief to a group of hardworking but imperiled blue-collar insects! I happened to be among those invited, and I was humbled by the broad range of concerned participants.

Beekeepers, nurserymen, botanical garden directors, wildlife habitat managers, and seed company CEOs were there to describe how they could help forge lasting solutions. The attendees of the summit were so diverse that I felt completely comfortable wearing my Franciscan habit rather than a business suit, which triggered a conversation about "caring for creation" with a few corporate CEOs who might otherwise have ignored me.

But what struck me most was the passion expressed by a rather heterogeneous set of business interests that we tend to monolithically label as Corporate America.

From Burt's Bees, the natural skincare line, to the AmericanHort alliance of nursery growers and landscapers, these companies and their professional associations clearly expressed commitment to the recovery of bees, monarch butterflies, and other floral visitors.

The battle cry from the White House's Office of Science and Technology policy was *"all hands on deck!"*

If farmers, their lobbyists, seed companies, and pesticide manufacturers did not feel welcomed to immediately engage in collaborative efforts on the ground, efforts to save monarchs and other pollinators were likely to fail.

But discussions of policy and practice could not be limited just to the big dogs in the ag industry. Most of the innovative pollinator habitat restoration efforts—and integrated pest- or weed-management practices—were emerging from small farmers and regional seed companies working with extension agents, nonprofits, and sustainable agriculture researchers.

And so we truly needed the involvement of both for-profits and non-profits, independent-minded organic farmers and the American Seed Trade Association—plus conservationists from the US, Mexico, and

Canada working across borders to recover threatened populations and restore international nectar corridors.

That's why Ina Warren and I formed the grassroots collaborative Make Way for Monarchs, guided and inspired by a dozen farmers and emotionally supported by the likes Homero Aridjis and Enriqueta Velarde from Mexico, David Suzuki and Margaret Atwood of Canada, and Barbara Kingsolver and Elizabeth Howard in the US.

To our surprise, our website received more than 2.5 million visits in its first two months, building on our efforts to get the word out in the *New York Times*, *Los Angeles Times*, and National Public Radio's *Living on Earth*.

That pollinators had come this far into the limelight was rather gratifying, but it also posed a problem for many conservationists used to going it alone or using litigation as their only tool. They debated whether the presence of the American Farm Bureau Federation, Bayer Crop Science, DuPont Pioneer, the National Corn Growers Association, and Syngenta at these meetings might help get the word out or would simply devolve into greenwashing without much action on the ground.

Some environmentalists were skeptical that the industry would add much to the discussion. But what if they were wrong? Couldn't these corporations, working in so-called conventional agriculture, help us forge viable solutions that farmers would be willing to adopt?

Along with Dr. Chip Taylor, founder of Monarch Watch, and Dr. Peter Raven, director emeritus of the Missouri Botanical Garden, I took a different tact. We requested appointments with various CEOs in the ag industry and accepted their invitations to meet with their coalitions that were trying to decide what roles they could play in pollinator recovery.

We all knew that we were coming from different cultures, but that did not preclude the possibility of finding common ground. Or courteously disagreeing with one another when our various goals did not immediately jive. We could always try again later.

Through a series of meetings on neutral ground in Chicago, Fort Collins, Portland, Querétaro, St. Louis, and Washington, DC, players from industry, farmers' organizations, academia, federal agencies, and nonprofits came together to work on collaborative strategies.

To be sure, not everyone was initially on the same page. Nevertheless, we agreed that our central goal had to be the health of pollinators and farmers themselves. If each of us demanded that our pet project or favored constituency be given priority, we would never get anywhere.

We also chose to focus on farmland where declines had historically been most precipitous. And we agreed that funding for habitat restoration and best management practices should be diversified and extended into multiyear projects that covered participating farmers' real out-of-pocket costs.

We did not pretend that pollinator recovery happens overnight or that it should be supported only with what cynics call "guilt money" from the industry.

If pollinator habitat restoration was to stick, it needed a funding base of private, federal, and philanthropic support, not just diverse players on the ground.

After deep engagement in this work for three years, I realized that my colleagues who "walked across the aisle" with me were never publically criticized by anyone from the ag industry. Even when there were grave differences, on everything from the language we used to the causes of the problem, most if not all participants were respectful enough to entertain views different from their own.

I suddenly realized that my brash stereotyping of those in the ag industry had not gotten me anywhere at all, simply because we had never been able to hear one another. As I learned more about my presumed "adversaries," their personal histories, their aspirations for their grandchildren, and their professional achievements, my views began to broaden.

I had to humbly admit that the ag industry's representatives were as heterogeneous and insightful as those from the environmental community.

These individuals were not necessarily "enemies of the environment" any more than the radical monkey-wrenching environmentalists I knew years ago were enemies of the state.

Regardless of what we think of the sometimes-strident rhetoric of either of these groups, I had to admit that it came from deep-seated values that deserved due consideration, even if they were somewhat different from my own.

Eventually, I retired from these policy debates to focus on restoration projects that I sensed would ultimately make a difference on the ground. But in a matter of three years, I witnessed major growth in the number and diversity of people engaged with on-farm pollinator habitat restoration.

When Ina Warren and I started Make Way for Monarchs, our modest goal was to recruit a board of eight farmers and beekeepers who had been successful in bringing back monarch butterflies and native bees to their fields and orchards. We wanted to honor and publicize their work as models of what other farmers could also accomplish.

Just two years later, I attended a meeting at the St. Louis Zoo of a national Monarch Collaborative. Not only were family farmers and stockmen there in the conference room with me, but so were officers of the national associations of soybean growers, corn growers, and wheat growers; farm bureau representatives; seed companies; pesticide producers and distributors; waterfowl and gamebird hunters; and habitat conservationists; as well as scientists from federal agencies and universities.

While I was inspired by the meeting, sooner or later I had to come back to what I could personally do on the ground. The first thing I did was plant a dozen kinds of milkweed as well as other pollinator-attracting wildflowers on our five acres.

Next, I wrote a USDA Sustainable Agriculture Research and Education grant to plant pollinator-attracting hedgerows around a dozen farms and gardens in a three-county area of Arizona, giving workshops to more than a hundred rural residents so that they could do the same.

When I realized that seed companies and nurseries were already being bought out of all of their milkweeds, I received two small grants to go on the road to collect seeds of eighteen different species of milkweed in four states in order to ramp up their nursery propagation.

This led me to create, with colleagues, a guide to milkweed supply chains, which went to every state highway department director in the nation, and another on pollinator plants of the Desert Southwest, which the USDA distributed for free to farmers, ranchers, nurserymen, and seed company employees across our region.

By that time, we began to take on monarch and bee habitat restoration work, collaborating with a dozen organizations, tribes, and federal agencies on both sides of the border. We held several bilingual training workshops on how to collect, propagate, and transplant milkweed as well as monitor monarchs.

These trainings and others by our collaborators reached more than twenty thousand people through more than 120 events. Many of the participants went home with milkweed seeds and other pollinator-attracting plants ready to set out in their gardens, fields, yards, and pastures.

All in all, participants in the Arizona Monarch Conservation Partnership propagated more than 15,600 native plants that serve as larval hosts or nectar sources for pollinators, including thirteen species of milkweed in less than two years. The partnership also restored butterfly habitat on 247 acres of public lands and 353 acres on private lands.

In Arizona, our alliance collectively developed twenty new Monarch Waystations that were registered on Monarch Watch, more than doubling the total in the entire state. We have also collaborated with and trained professionals who manage tribal lands, protected areas, museum grounds, and schoolyard gardens in New Mexico, Texas, Baja California, Sonora, Chihuahua, Coahuila, Nuevo Leon, Querétaro, Aguascalientes, and Sinaloa.

Nationally, literally hundreds of organizations have joined in the work of on-ground pollinator restoration. The Xerces Society has already collaborated with local organizations to train more than seventy thousand farmers and ranchers in restoring, planting, and managing on-farm pollinator habitat.

Beginning in 2010 but accelerating since 2015, these land managers have begun the restoration of pollinator habitats on more than ten thousand acres of Conservation Stewardship (CSP) lands, 463,000 acres of Conservation Reserve (CRP) lands, and 97,000 acres of Environmental Quality Incentive program (EQIP) lands.

In November 2016, the USDA Natural Resource Conservation Service, General Mills, and the Xerces Society agreed to work together to plant or restore another two hundred thousand acres of pollinator habitat by 2020. More is to come.

To be sure, we cannot attribute these successes to any one individual, organization, funding source, culture or nation. *That is just the point.*

To make a clear disclaimer, while Steve Buchmann and I worked to catalyze some pioneering efforts toward pollinator restoration, I have rarely served as a leader or manager of these initiatives. The credit should go to folks like Mace Vaughn, Catherine Werner, Stephen Buchmann, Nathalie Chambers, Laura Jackson, Carol Davit, Loretta McGrath, Sergio Avila, Ina Warren, Gail Morris, Francesca Claverie, Trecia Neal, Chip Taylor, Guadalupe Malda, and Eric Mader.

In their own ways, each of these individuals has taken action on the ground to help butterflies, hummingbirds, and bats continue their long journeys. These species, traveling hundreds or even thousands of miles each year, need a seamless corridor for their migrations, with "safe harbor" sanctuaries for use as stopovers throughout their three-country range.

Only when we work together, across borders, can we assure the fate of these "Dreamers" of the animal world.

We know instinctively that pollinators are valuable, but in conservation work, it can help to quantify that value. Some of the brightest ecologists working in the field today are doing just that, from Claire Kremen in California and Rachael Winfree in New Jersey to Hannah Burrack in North Carolina as well as large teams in Burkina Faso and Germany.

They have confirmed that when wild bees and honeybees pollinate food crops, it increases the quantity and quality of that crop, from blueberries to sesame to almonds. The diversity of wild bee species on a farm or orchard turns out to be a better indicator of pollinator effectiveness on some food crops than simply the gross number of bees.

As Hannah Burrack and her colleagues at North Carolina State University have determined, farmers gain an extra $311 per acre of fruit yields for each additional bee group near highbush blueberry patches. Hannah argues that her state's blueberry industry gains immense benefit each time restoration efforts bring back at least one more species of bee.

In fact, Hannah pegs the pollination value of each additional bee group colonizing blueberry patches in North Carolina at $1.42 million each year.

Of course, the best way to sustain healthy populations of bees and other pollinators is by restoring toxin-free habitats in and near fields and orchards. So let's ask a final question about the value of pollinator recovery efforts.

Regardless of whether we taste the fruits of these labors, do they actually save pollinators to the degree that they no longer require inclusion on endangered species lists?

The answer to this question is a work in progress and may vary greatly with the kind of pollinator and the kind of threat. One of the most hopeful stories we have is of the lesser long-nosed bat, *Leptonycteris yerbabuenae*, a pollinator that was once listed as endangered in both the US and Mexico. Not only was it delisted in 2017, but it is now on its way toward further population recovery.

How? Through two decades of diligent efforts to discover, monitor, and protect seventy-five of its roosts in Mexico and the US. But the new hope from here on out is bat population enhancement through the innovative adoption of bat-friendly practices on tequila and mezcal plantations in Mexico.

The logic of this innovation goes something like this. The agaves or century plants that are used to make mezcal and tequila have multiple pollinators that facilitate their reproduction.

But just one of these pollinators, the lesser long-nosed bat, pollinates 30 to 90 percent of any given plant population, for it appears to be acutely coevolved with agave blossoms. Using their long, brush-tipped tongues, these little (25 g) bats gain nutrition from the nectar and pollen of night-blooming flowers of desert cacti and succulents like agaves.

But there is an additional factor to consider: agaves can, when needed, reproduce on their own, cloning sideshoots called *hijuelos* that can be separated and transplanted like so many bulblets in a clump of bunching onions. In fact, thousands of genetically identical clonal agave plants can be put out over an entire field.

Lesser long-nosed bats appear to require nectar from about 250 to 300 cactus flowers or agave blossoms to fuel their migration from central Mexico to their northernmost summer haunts in New Mexico and Arizona. In certain parts of the bats' migratory corridor, wild agaves used for mezcal production are seldom allowed to flower and fruit before they are harvested. Those flowerless plants can disrupt bat migration and diminish their *reproductive* success.

Beginning in the early seventies, as margaritas became more popular, agave production increased in the *zona tequilera* of Jalisco and Nayarit largely by cloning one genetically narrow strain of *tequila azul*. Those highly valued plants almost never flowered before being harvested for tequila. Neither did wild agaves nearby. A rather wide swath of western Mexico lost much of the nectar needed by long-nosed bats.

By the early 1980s we knew that restoration was needed if the lesser long-nosed bat was to thrive. One of the first proposals was to encourage Mexican agave harvesters to let a certain percentage of plants flower within their reach (and that of the bats).

By the late 1990s, this proposal was at last taken seriously by the Migratory Pollinator Conservation team that included Rodrigo Medellin from the National Autonomous University of Mexico, Steve Walker of Bat Conservation International, those of us working at Arizona-Sonora Desert Museum, and several of our colleagues doing innovative research in Jalisco, which is ground zero for the tequila industry.

Some of us went so far as to visit the Tequila Producers Chamber of Commerce in Guadalajara to talk with leaders in the industry about this proposal, but they showed little initial interest. Bat Conservation International then piloted a project with *Tequila Chamucos* to test-market a special run of their tequila with labels featuring a gaggle of bats. We hoped the distillery could offer a percentage of its earnings to BCI for bat conservation education.

And yet it seemed at the time that there was still more urgent, fundamental work to be done to save bats and diversify agaves. Through no one's fault, the concept went dormant for a while.

Fortunately, one member of that team—award-winning zoologist Rodrigo Medellin—had the tenacity and insight to reshape the modest proposal into something far more viable and visible. He did so by entertaining some rather interesting prospects: Why not certify bat-friendly practices that mezcal and tequila producers could undertake to give them a larger market share? Why not ask the growers to allow just 3 to 5 percent of their agave plants—roughly 220 per hectare—to flower? Why not see if these blossoms could provide bats with an additional source of nectar and a bit more genetic diversity to plants to guard against droughts, pests, and diseases?

I'm sure that Rodrigo's eloquence was part of what won the agave growers over. But they probably also well remembered the $20 million of losses in 1999 alone due to fungal and bacterial diseases.

Nicknamed TMA—*Tristeza y Muerte de Agave*—the cocktail of pathogens infected at least 40 percent of all the plants in *tequila azul* plantations and killed off at least a quarter of them during the worst years. It was the kind of epidemic triggered by crop genetic uniformity that Ana Valenzuela and I had predicted in the mid-1990s when few in the industry would listen to our warnings.

Were the producers willing to risk the consequences of genetic uniformity again, just as the international markets for both mezcals and tequilas were surging?

But the real difference that could make Bat Friendly Tequila and Mezcal a success this time around was that Rodrigo built a robust collaboration to support it. He partnered with Guadalajara-born entrepreneur David Suro-Piñera of Philadelphia to form the Tequila Interchange Project (TIP). It has become a platform that welcomed players in every link of the agave supply chain to promote Bat Friendly beverages.

As Rodrigo soon announced, "Today, for the first time ever, academics, producers, distillers, bottlers, marketers, and bartenders are joining forces to produce Bat Friendly Tequila and Mezcal and to defend the agave, its pollinators, and Mexico's national drinks."

First one distillery came on, then another. Then another. Tequila Ocho. Siete Leguas. Tequila Tapatio. Tequila Cascahuin. Siembra Valles Ancestral. Thanks to David Suro's knowledge of the American beverage industry, cutting-edge mixologists began to feature products from these microdistillers and their medium-sized cousins.

At first, it was the small-batch tequila producers who owned their own fields who could shift their farming practices with more agility, leaving agaves to flower in the hedgerows edging their plantations.

And soon, to many biologists' surprise, the TIP supporters collected more than three hundred thousand viable seeds of cross-pollinated agaves from one plantation alone, now stored for future planting at the Camarena family distillery.

As other farmers relaxed enough to let 3 to 5 percent of their agaves flower as they had historically done in Jalisco, Rodrigo and his colleagues realized they had already harvested more than a million agave seeds from lands that had probably not produced a single seed from a century plant in over a century!

Not only were bats coming back into the agave fields to move pollen and imbibe nectar, but the resulting seeds could be used to diversify future plantings.

In Medellin's mind, the entire story is about forging lasting partnerships not only between bats and agaves but between people of different countries, cultural backgrounds, and skill sets: "It's really important to note that this was an effort [accomplished] by a lot of people in Mexico and the United States [to be of benefit] for both bats and business. It's a great example of how partnering *can* work."

But Medellin is something like a rolling stone with a mind that never sleeps and with eyes that continue to look for other opportunities, rather than resting on his laurels: "There is more than enough work to be carried out in the foreseeable future in the bat conservation arena . . . We have taken [only] the first steps, and now the program requires solid strategic planning, numerous participants, and a dependable collaborative scheme. Never have the circumstances and situations been more promising to achieve bat conservation; never will it be more feasible and timely than now."

CHAPTER 13

You Can Go Home Again

Have you ever recognized someone at a farmers' market whom you had seen years before, when she stood alone on a street corner, unemployed and desperate to make money off what she could sell out of a single cooler?

And yet now, as you look at her, do you see that she is surrounded by allegiant customers eager to make their weekly purchase of a wide range of hand-harvested, homemade foods?

Have you noticed someone else, picking a basketful of fruit in a city park or along a treelined bike trail, where orchard trees were intentionally planted so that their fruits can be accessible to anyone?

Have you met someone at a church dinner who admitted that, until recently, he had been incarcerated but now felt ready to reenter the local workforce? I can bet that you were surprised—like I have been—when that person introduced himself by proudly proclaiming something like "Hi, my name is Jose, and I need your help. If I'm lucky enough to graduate from my job-training program, I'm hoping I'll find a way to become an urban farmer. I'll need prayers and some start-up support from all of you!"

I want to express my own hope that individuals like these will ultimately be those who most benefit from collaborations to restore America's food-producing landscapes. It is they who have been most marginalized by our industrialized, depersonalized food system. And often they are also the very people who bring the rest of us our daily bread—the migrant farmworker, the fishmonger, the oysterman, the food service worker, the short-order cook, and the waitress.

They are the ones most likely to need food relief from a soup kitchen, church pantry, or food bank to feed themselves and their children. Furthermore, it is not a given that they will benefit from efforts to change our food system, no matter how many food justice advocates are working in their community.

This cruel irony makes my heart ache, for despite all the good work accomplished by the "slow food movement" over the last twenty years, I fear that it has not always helped those most in need, those who deserve better.

I want to make one point exceedingly clear: *the grinding poverty that we see in so many urban and rural communities cannot be solved by food restoration projects if they exist in a socioeconomic vacuum.* The benefits of top-down food restoration projects will no more "trickle down" to the poor than corporate tax breaks will. If you simply offer food relief or even temporary employment to a low-income family without ever addressing the root causes of their poverty and structural inequities, they may well end up hungry again.

We cannot vanquish poverty by bread alone.

But if done right, community-based restoration projects can offer more than just food. Their collaborative, inclusive processes can set the stage for social and economic benefits to reach those once disempowered and impoverished by our commodified food economy, becoming a positive force moving us toward larger, more lasting solutions.

In this spirit, let me take a few moments to describe one set of initiatives, in one still-impoverished community, that has given me hope. In expressing my optimism about them, I am not implying that we can yet claim any long-term successes. Instead, I am merely describing how various food projects are weaving a stronger safety net for those who were previously hitting the ground with nothing at all to buffer them from the hard realities they had fallen upon.

On December 11, 2015, the United Nations Educational, Scientific, and Cultural Organization (UNESCO) designated Tucson, Arizona, as the first "City of Gastronomy" in the US. That day, Tucson's mayor Jonathan Rothschild agreed to join 115 other metro areas in 54 countries as members of the Creative Cities Network sponsored by the United Nations.

At the press conference in City Hall that December, Mayor Rothschild described the 4,100-year history of food production in the Tucson Basin—the oldest continuous agricultural tradition in any metro area in the US. More important, perhaps, the mayor also suggested that this honor could help reduce the prevailing poverty and food insecurity in the community. I seconded his motion in my brief comments to the press that day, arguing that we needed to use this recognition to coalesce our resources and build on existing efforts to relieve hunger, obesity, and diabetes. That will ultimately be our litmus test.

Many Tucsonans cheered this announcement, for it had been some time since Arizona in general and Tucson in particular had received much positive press. Tucsonans needed some good news, something else to be proud of.

While we celebrated that designation, fewer than two years later, President Trump officially pulled the US out of UNESCO. Remarkably, because of the safety net we had begun to build, the withdrawal has hardly affected collaborations within our metro area or among other metro areas we now refer to as *cities of food cultures*.

Still, the Old Pueblo had lagged behind other cities in recovering from the Great Recession and had been recently beleaguered by several tragic events, including the assassination attempt on US congresswoman Gabby Gifford that killed several other people. As late as 2015, the American Community Survey indicated that poverty levels inside Tucson's city limits remained staggeringly high (24 percent) compared to its surrounding metro area of Pima County (18 percent) and to the state of Arizona as a whole (16 percent).

So Tucsonans were thirsting for something to celebrate, a positive effort to get behind. At last, the many innovative nonprofits, businesses, and educational institutions in our area were being recognized for their good work. Up to $13 million worth of free press, radio, television, and social media coverage of Tucson's food cultures began to roll in that day, with fresh stories featured each and every month for the following two years.

And yet, as the initial excitement subsided, many Tucsonans found that the phrase "City of Gastronomy" did not roll very easily off their tongues.

"What does that mean we are?" my neighbors asked. "A city of gourmets and gourmands? A city with a thriving food scene? A city with deep food history?"

"Or does it mean we want to become a city with lots of fancy restaurants? Hell, most of our families can't afford to eat in a sit-down restaurant more than once a month!"

At the Food Justice Forum a couple months later, where the mayor launched Tucson's role in the UNESCO network, one Chicana activist had the candor to ask, "How will the dishwasher in a fast food restaurant feel any different about what she or he does because of this designation?"

That question was well put—in fact, powerfully and painfully so. To be sure, most Arizona cities had been struggling ever since the triple whammy of the Great Recession, the massive subprime mortgage scandal, and our state government's rancorous immigration policies that had ravaged the economy.

But that may have been the very reason that UNESCO temporarily bypassed applications from better-known "food cities" like Portland,

Seattle, and New Orleans to focus on Tucson. Those cities had federal redevelopment funds, philanthropic gifts, and impact investments, while Tucson had few of these incentives.

Without other options, our community used grassroots innovations to deal with our challenges. Those challenges included severe poverty, water scarcity, high public-health costs, the need to create green jobs, the necessity of diverting still-edible food out of the waste stream, and the urge to celebrate our unique multicultural food traditions without cultural appropriation.

In letters of support for the UNESCO designation, Tucson's many food and farming entrepreneurs did not claim they had already fixed the city's social, economic, and nutritional problems. Such problems had been plaguing Old Pueblo and other borderland cities for decades and had deep roots.

Instead, our food nonprofits and grassroots alliances showed that they had taken small but tangible steps toward change. They were fostering the kind of innovations that often begin on the margins of a power structure, fine-tuning them so that they would gain greater traction as others join in. After these initiatives achieve a modicum of success, they are often blessed and financially supported by more prominent organizations and civic leaders so that they can spread more rapidly.

One of Tucson's most beloved examples is the adoption of "curb-cutting": allowing storm water from the city's paved streets to flow into basins placed between the street and the sidewalk where edible trees can be irrigated. This practice began with our "Harvest Rain" guru, Brad Lancaster, around 1998, when he began to capture rainwater from his street front, roof, and other hard surfaces. He now stores one hundred thousand gallons every year in his small yard, providing all the irrigation needed for dozens of edible trees in the heart of the city.

At one point early on, Brad and his brother were nearly arrested for cutting curbs without permits. But within three years (by 2001),

Lancaster had worked with the city to legalize the process and get block grants to help one neighborhood after another transition their provision of moisture to desert landscaping to harvested rainwater.

Lancaster used back-of-the-envelope calculations to convince policy-makers that their blessing could have real payoffs for a place like Tucson, which rarely receives more than ten inches of annual rainfall anymore. Outdoor landscaping was consuming more than a quarter of all water piped by the city's utility to residential lots, so if another source could reduce that demand, the savings would be great. When Brad calculated the volume of rainfall hitting Tucson's residential streets, he found that the water harvested from a mile stretch of pavement was enough to fully meet the water demands of four hundred maturing fruit trees.

The policymakers were convinced it was worth a try. The city offered residents a $500 to $2,000 rebate to transition their landscaping from pumped and piped groundwater to harvested rainwater. After five years, the program had doled out $2 million to residents and businesses, but the payoff has been worth the investment. Property owners participating in the program each save an average of 748 gallons of piped water every year.

At the same time, this grassroots movement has created enormous demand for gutters, cisterns, and drip irrigation systems that have reduced overall water use even more than the amount of rainwater being captured. Just one of Tucson's many nurseries and hardware stores sell more than a million dollars of cisterns and other kinds of water storage tanks in the average year.

Training workshops and demonstrations on water harvesting tech-niques were soon cropping up everywhere within our metro area. In addition, several new microenterprises began to help residents install water-harvesting and small irrigation systems in order to maintain their edible landscapes.

But just where were all those desert-adapted edibles going to come from? Most hardware stores and garden centers in the US today sell the same water-guzzling plants from coast to coast. In contrast, Tucsonans have long prided themselves on their use of native desert plants, and the availability of edible natives had gradually increased in our nurseries, public gardens, and restaurants.

At least five seed banks and several sizeable nurseries had established large followings: the USDA NRCS Plant Materials Center, the Arizona-Sonora Desert Museum, Native Seeds/SEARCH, Pima County Parks and Recreation Nursery, and the Desert Legume Project (DELEP). Native Seeds/SEARCH in particular had been active in providing small samples of seeds to school gardens, tribal farms, indigenous agricultural interns, immigrant relief projects, and other public institutions in the area. It is ranked fifth in the nation among both nonprofit and for-profit seed outlets in terms of the conservation value and diversity of its edible offerings.

So when the Pima County Public Library proposed establishing free seed libraries, using old card files to house garden packets at each one of its twenty-some branches in the Tucson Basin, many of these seed banks and nurseries simply offered the librarians every plant they felt could grow in Tucson! Within a couple years, librarians such as Justine Hernandez and Kelly Wilson had created the largest free seed interlibrary loan program in the country.

In short order, more than 2,500 seed accessions were "checked out" by home gardeners and members of Tucson's twenty-four community gardens, fifty-seven school gardens, and refugees' gardens. The librarians were heartened to learn that 60 percent of people who checked out the packets returned at least some seed after harvest time to replenish the stocks available to others the next season.

Other groups joined in too. Trees for Tucson donated more than seven thousand trees bearing edible fruits, nuts, or pods to be planted in low-income neighborhoods, affordable housing developments, and on prison grounds. Three nonprofits—Desert Survivors Nursery, Mission Gardens, and Tohono Chul Park—as well as the family-owned Civano Nursery provided dozens of other fruit varieties through their collaborations with schools and nonprofits.

While other cities may have a few analogous programs, Tucson has sown an entire ecosystem to share seeds with families living below the poverty level. Food plant vendors made sure their offerings could be purchased with EBT cards, allowing families to use their SNAP benefits not just to buy a single meal but to grow fruits and vegetables for many meals.

What developed next was a surprise to many involved in seed and plant marketing. Several dozen desert-adapted varieties began to appear at swap meets, flea markets (*pulgas*), *tianguis*, and street fairs for remarkably affordable prices. They had been propagated on back porches, in empty cans of baby formula, beer, or cooking oil, and sold on fold-up card tables.

By the summer of 2017, Tucsonans had local access to more than 2,020 named varieties of 130 cultivated annual food crops; 140 species of wild, native desert edible plants; and more than 200 varieties of domesticated fruit, nut, berry, and succulent edibles. Families who needed free or discounted prices could obtain 80 percent of the annual food plants and 20 percent of the perennial fruit, nut, berry, and tuber plants in the city. This level of affordable access to food biodiversity is unprecedented in most metro areas in North America.

If that were the end of the story, you might feel dazzled by the numbers but still dumbfounded by the high levels of unemployment, underemployment, food insecurity, obesity, and diabetes that have persisted in Metro Tucson. But fortunately, it is not the end.

Young entrepreneurs—from wild foragers and farmers to millers, bakers, tortilla makers, cactus syrup processers, distillers, brewers, *mole* makers, mixologists, and fermenters—have begun to use these local ingredients to develop new products, most of them unique to Tucson or the border region.

By last count, we now have more than 140 new products circulating in Tucson's markets, festivals, gift shops, microbreweries, and restaurants, prepared by more than forty start-ups, most of which did not exist even five years ago. Forty microenterprises—most of them younger than five years old at the time of this writing—now employ hundreds of food growers, foragers, and processors who had been hard-pressed to garner livable wages doing what they most loved. In addition, fourteen locally owned microbreweries in Tucson now use heritage grains or wild forms from our area in their beers.

Many customers learned about these opportunities through our flagship publication, *Edible Baja Arizona*. During the bimonthly magazine's four-year run, each edition offered 150 to 180 pages of information to seventy thousand local readers. More than 170 local businesses regularly placed ads for their locally sourced products and events.

Residents in Tucson came to realize that they could "taste the uniqueness of our place" in a dozen different ways, not just one. And the magazine often featured stories of people who were working for food security and social justice.

By 2016, we began to see some positive trends in Tucson's food business sector for the first time in almost a decade. The region's biodiverse foods were triggering some of the financial recovery in an otherwise lagging local economy. In the Pima County landscape that surrounds Metro Tucson, the Health Department documented a 6 percent increase in restaurants; a 6 percent increase in food markets; a 12 percent increase in mobile food vendors; a 12 percent increase in food distributors; a 14 percent increase in food processors and manufacturers; a 24 percent increase in caterers; and a 26 percent increase in bars, microbreweries, and distilleries.

Using just about any measure, it is clear that *the 2016 food economy grew faster than any other economic sector in Tucson*, creating both livelihoods and nourishment. As my colleague Jonathan Mabry has noted, Tucson has more than 1,200 restaurants and bars, which employ more than thirty thousand people. Almost two-thirds (63 percent) of these establishments are locally owned, nonchain businesses. When grocery stores are included, food businesses provide 14 percent of all jobs in the city. That is all very good news for our economy.

These positive trends are now readily visible on our streets and in our swap meets, not just in the gift shops of resort hotels and in fancy restaurants. Tucson and its Pima County suburbs harbor twelve times the number of mobile food trucks and carts as New York City. Some 941 nomadic food entrepreneurs roam around the county, some registered with the city, some not.

As many as 235 full-service food carts, 45 *dogero* pushcarts, and 85 nomadic caterers stationed themselves along the dusty streets of Tucson and the roughly paved rural routes coming into the metro area. And in January 2018, a former *dogero* known as the Guero Canelo became the fourth Tucsonan to receive a James Beard Award. His was for bringing the delicious and affordable Sonoran hot dog to national attention.

Bright young people in Tucson, like Jamaican American Haile Thomas, are getting palpably excited about becoming chefs and food entrepreneurs. The number of culinary arts programs in the area has doubled, reaching twenty-one by 2016.

One training program, La Caridad Kitchen of the Community Food Bank, graduated 118 students from its ten-week course. The same food bank provided training for nearly twenty thousand other individuals in food production, processing, and nutrition.

A few miles away from the food bank, a social justice collective, *Flowers and Bullets*, has garnered more than $600,000 of public support to create a nine-acre midtown farm and food justice training center in the

Hispanic neighborhood known as Barrio Centro. The kitchen and urban farm are just two of at least twenty nonprofit food justice efforts that have emerged in the Old Pueblo.

Together, these groups have begun to reinvigorate the debate about Tucson's food future by involving just about every race, culture, political persuasion, and faith—immigrant and native, documented and undocumented—found in our community.

I love all these good statistics, but what makes me most hopeful is that much of this progress was accomplished by industrious individuals who began with little capital but expansive visions. They have put their energy into rainwater harvesting, hothouse gardening, vertical farming, wild foraging, making mesquite tortillas or planting heritage trees, gleaning fallen fruits or fermenting greens into sauerkraut, learning the ropes of managing a community kitchen, or selling vegetable transplants at a swap meet.

Their roles are so much more varied than simply being a grass-fed cattle rancher, an heirloom corn farmer, or a celebrity chef. It is this diversity of voices and choices that is making Tucson live up to its status as the first "City of Food Cultures" in the United States.

The people working in these collaborations are well aware of the divisiveness that surrounds them. They can see how polarization is undermining our federal government, crippling our state governments, anesthetizing our foundations, and diminishing the compassionate responses of our educational institutions.

And yet most Tucson residents are choosing collaboration over competition to get our food system back on track. They have found novel ways to create—from the grassroots up—a series of striking innovations that not only have begun to feed our community members who are most in need but have offered them a new range of livelihoods.

It is fair to say that they are now being nourished by food from the radical center, perhaps because they are reengaged with many of their neighbors who are also taking the middle path.

There's a certain irony to all this. While few university economists or community development wonks were even paying attention, Tucsonans of all stripes jump-started an economic recovery through food recovery. How? Because, as studies commissioned by Local First Arizona have shown, seventy-three cents of every dollar spent with independently owned food businesses stays in our community, compared with only forty-three cents of every dollar spent at national franchises. Today, it appears that less money is draining away from our community to corporate headquarters in other states.

And while ranchers and environmentalists were still duking it out in the hinterlands of Nevada, Oregon, Utah, and West Texas, at least five landscape-level coalitions of urban consumers and rural livestock producers have emerged in Arizona, bringing innovative restaurants like Diablo Burger to both Tucson and Flagstaff. Such locally owned and sourced businesses have become the "face" of the radical center.

This, to me, is the ultimate value of community-based food restoration: it builds goodwill that spills over into other parts of our society.

Yes, these projects have surely recovered a variety of edible plants, fish, and game. But more than that, they have begun to heal old wounds so that other pressing problems can be addressed.

I hear this sense of hope in the words of my friend Chris Bianco, one of the award-winning chefs who has been most engaged with small growers and nonprofits in our region. I think Chris captures the feeling shared by many in Tucson about how collaborative work changes more than just what we see on our dinner plate: "You know, what has changed my life is the daily act, filled with best intentions, of working with all of these people—farmers, ranchers, millers, cheesemakers, tomato canners—for they have become more than mere suppliers; they have become my friends."

The metaphor of nourishing relationships can be extended to everyone who touches or is touched by the foods and food-producing lands that individuals like you have all helped recover and restore. By reaching out to your neighbors, being needed by them and needing their goodwill yourself, you are among those who are slowly fermenting the next revolution. It is my prayer that your efforts will keep building, rising, and raising all of us up—like a leavened ball of dough—to become a more richly textured world where we may eat all together at a common table.

The Conservation Couplets

A Manifesto for Moving from Top-Down Protectionism to Bottom-Up Community-Based Restoration

WE ONCE FEARED THAT *"the world is doomed and the selfish actions of the earth's many people are what is dooming it."*

We can see now that *"if humans have the capacity to wound the earth, we also have the capacity to heal it. We have the humility to recognize, utilize, and to celebrate our collective healing capacity, and to somehow be healed ourselves by participating in that restoration process."*

We once self-righteously felt that *"we have to demand an immediate fix to environmental problems to force others to respond who cannot immediately see the necessity of doing so."*

We now understand that *"we need to make change happen by working* with *others and changing ourselves. We need to include others in envisioning and implementing shifts toward a more inclusive set of players."*

* * *

We once passed judgment that *"destructive human behaviors need to be constrained so urgently that top-down regulation* must *become the most expedient and dominant means of protecting the environment and saving species."*

We now concede that *"our tool kit of conservation and restoration strategies will need to offer far more options than regulation, restriction, and punitive actions. Instead, we will need to unleash our personal and collective capacities to foster fresh innovation at the same time we honor cultural traditions and voluntary practices of self-restraint."*

We once assumed that *"placing more wildlands and waters under the management authority of government agencies will allow us to avoid the tragedy of the commons."*

We must now admit that *"comanagement with local communities can level the playing field. Why? Top-down command-and-control management of resources and landscapes by bureaucracies can often disenfranchise or bankrupt local communities' capacities as long-term stakeholders. Tragically, it has resulted in pushback from local communities and even armed conflict or clandestine destruction of resources conservationists had hoped to protect."*

We once presumed that *"hunting and fishing by the poor and hungry are killing off the earth's fish and wildlife, so we have to been forced to protect* nature from *people in order to prevent the overharvesting that will extirpate species if left unchecked."*

Today, we are delighted by the successes that are achieved when *"we positively reengage people in supporting the processes of nature rather than isolating them from other species and nature's own regenerative processes. At the same time, we must acknowledge that the loss of plants and microbes due to chemical and physical fragmentation of habitats and landscapes is now imperiling more biodiversity than is hunting and fishing of vertebrate animals."*

* * *

We once felt inclined to *"write off the conservation value of disturbed, anthropogenic, and cultural managed habitats as well as the value of domesticated species. We opted for investing only in the protection of wilderness and the remaining diversity of wild, untrammeled species."*

We now feel emboldened to *"engage people of all ages, races, and classes in the restoration of diversity in culturally managed landscapes. That includes embracing the recovery of diversity in the cultivated crops, managed livestock, and fermentation microbes that are essential to regenerative agriculture and healthy diets. Some community-based initiatives begun in degraded habitats may now allow us to test restoration methods, which we may someday use in more pristine habitats."*

We once fatalistically asserted that *"poor minorities in urban areas and indigenous communities in the hinterlands often become the victims of hazardous wastes and other contamination. That is because they have yet to develop the economic power, political standing, or environmental leadership capacity that will keep bad things from happening in their midsts."*

We now relish that fact that *"people of color are not inevitably victims; they are valued leaders in and essential to our broader society's efforts to care for creation. That may be because they so deeply express their sacred duty to integrate social justice and environmental quality issues to ensure the wellbeing of their families and communities for the next seven generations and for all of humankind."*

We once believed that *"science alone should be enough to ensure the rational management and wise use of natural resources for the public good."*

We now humbly recognize that *"scientists, policy makers, and on-ground resource managers need to be in constant dialogue with ethicists, faith-based communities, and culture bearers. If we ignore the need for dialogue between science and the spirit, we will not be able to achieve just, equitable, and morally appropriate means to care for creation and for the poor still strug-gling in our midst."*

We once held that *"biological conservation is about the rescue and relega-tion of imperiled species to be protected in fortress-like parks, zoos, botanical gardens, and seed banks."*

We now sense that *"lasting biological conservation comes from restoring relationships among plants, animals, and microbial populations in a gradi-ent of habitats that all include both natural and cultural elements."*

Economists once warned us that *"conservation will cost so much money and jobs that the growth of local and regional economies will inevitably be slowed, disrupted, or diminished."*

It has become evident that *"cooperative restoration strategies generate more livelihoods with livable wages, valuable ecosystem services, and local multiplier effects. These can be done in a manner that sustains local assets and enhances regional economies so that they become less vulnerable to exter-nal threats and more resilient in the face of uncertainty."*

We once blindly accepted the premise that *"wildlife conservation and economic use simply do not mix. Why restore a species to its habitat, then hunt or fish it? Instead, we should take shots not with guns but with cameras. We should protect charismatic megafauna as watchable wildlife in accessible reserves where people can see them. These flagship species will allow 'trickle-down' conservation to be achieved."*

We might be better served by *"broadening our focus to conserve and restore all sorts of wild and cultivated species, including microbes, plants, and animals. There is no good ethical reason that we should not pay particular attention to safeguarding and enjoying the very species that bring us our daily bread. They also provide many of nature's services that keep our watersheds, airsheds, and foodsheds functioning for other species as well."*

Literature Cited

Title page quotes are from Andrew C. Revkin (2015) in his essay "Restoring the Nature of America," in Ben A. Minteer and Stephen J. Pyne, eds., *After Preservation: Saving American Nature in the Age of Humans*, University of Chicago Press, Chicago, IL, 12; and from Charles F. Wilkinson (2014) in his foreword to Susan Charnley, Thomas E. Sheridan, and Gary P. Nabhan, eds., *Stitching the West Back Together: Conservation of Working Landscapes*, University of Chicago Press, Chicago, IL, xi.

Introduction: Conservation You Can Taste

Aronson, James, Suzanne J. Milton, and James N. Blignaut, eds. 2007. *Natural Capital: Science, Business and Practice*. Island Press, Washington, DC.

BenDor, Todd, T. William Lester, Avery Livengood, Adam Davis, and Logan Yonavjak. 2015. Estimating the Size and Impact of the Ecological Restoration Economy. *PLOS ONE* 10(6): 0128339. http://journals.plos.org/plosone/article?id=10.1371/journal.pone.0128339.

Charnley, Susan, Thomas E. Sheridan, and Gary P. Nabhan, eds. *Stitching the West Back Together: Conservation of Working Landscapes*. University of Chicago Press, Chicago, IL.

Chinni, Dante, and James Gimpel. 2011. *Our Patchwork Nation*. Avery Books, New York, NY.

Dukes, E. Franklin, Karen E. Frederick, and Juliana E. Birkhof, eds. 2011. *Community-Based Collaboration: Bridging Socio-ecological Research and Practice*. University of Virginia Press, Charlottesville, VA.

Ehrlich, Gretel. 1989. Commentary in G. P. Nabhan, ed. *Enduring Seeds*. North Point Press, San Francisco, CA.

Friederici, Peter. 2006. *Nature's Restoration: People and Places on the Front Lines of Conservation*. Shearwater Books/Island Press, Washington, DC.

Hawken, Paul. 2007. *Blessed Unrest: How the Largest Movement in the World Came into Being and Why No One Saw It Coming*. Viking/Penguin Group, Washington, DC.

Kasich, John, and David Paisner. 2017. *Two Paths: America Divided or United*. Thomas Dunne Books, New York, NY.

Meine, Curt, and Gary P. Nabhan. 2014. Historic Precedents to Collaborative Conservation in Working Landscapes: The Coon Valley "Cooperative Conservation" Initiative. In Susan Charnley, Thomas E. Sheridan, and Gary P. Nabhan, eds., *Stitching the West Back Together: Conservation of Working Landscapes* (pp. 77–80). University of Chicago Press, Chicago, IL.

Zwick, Steve. 2017, September 22. Ten Things You Need to Know about the Restoration Economy. *Ecosystem Marketplace*. http://www.greenbiz.com/steve/zwick-o.

Chapter One. A Land Divided

Bishop, Bill. 2008. *The Big Sort: Why the Clustering of Like-Minded America Is Tearing Us Apart*. Houghton-Mifflin, Boston, MA.

Brewer, Marillynn B., and Norman Miller. 1996. *Intergroup Relations*. Brooks/Cole, Pacific Grove, CA.

Broeckhaven, Nicky, and An Cliquet. 2015. Gender and Ecological Restoration: Time to Connect the Dots. *Restoration Ecology* 23(6): 729–736.

Chinni, Dante, and James Gimpel. 2011. *Our Patchwork Nation*. Avery Books, New York, NY.

Marty, Martin E. 2004, August 4. *The Greatest Divide*. https://divinity.uchicago.edu/sightings/greatest-divide-%E2%80%94-martin-e-marty.

McNeil, Brenda Salter. 2015. *Roadmap to Reconciliation: Moving Communities into Unity, Wholeness and Justice*. IVP Books, Downers Grove, IL.

Pew Center. 2015. *Perception of Conflict between Science and Religion*. http://www.pewinternet.org/2015/10/22/perception-of-conflict-between-science-and-religion/.

Pew Center. 2017. *For Earth Day, Here's How Americans View Environmental Issues*. http://www.pewresearch.org/fact-tank/2017/04/20/for-earth-day-heres-how-americans-view-environmental-issues/.

Purdy, Jedidiah. 2015. *After Nature: A Politics for the Anthropocene*. Harvard University Press, Cambridge, MA.

Putnam, Robert D. 2000. *Bowling Alone: The Collapse and Revival of American Communities*. Simon and Shuster, New York, NY.

Walker, Bruce. 2012, August 16. The Decline of Greenism. *The American Thinker*. http://www.americanthinker.com/articles/2012/04/the_decline _of_greenism_comments.html.

Wines, Michael, and John Schwartz. 2016, February 9. Unsafe Lead Levels in Tap Water Not Limited to Flint. *New York Times*.

Chapter Two. Farming in the Radical Center

Dukes, E. Franklin. 2011. The Promise of Community-Based Collaboration: Agenda for an Authentic Future. In E. Franklin Dukes, Karen E. Frederick, and Juliana E. Birkhof, eds., *Community-Based Collaboration: Bridging Socio-ecological Research and Practice* (pp. 189–215). University of Virginia Press, Charlottesville, VA.

Marais, Christo, et al. 2007. Overcoming Socioeconomic Obstacles to Restoring Natural Capital. In James Aronson, Suzanne J. Milton, and James N. Blignaut, eds., *Natural Capital: Science, Business and Practice* (pp. 256–264). Island Press, Washington, DC.

McNeil, Brenda Salter. 2015. *Roadmap to Reconciliation: Moving Communities into Unity, Wholeness and Justice*. IVP Books, Downers Grove, IL.

Nabhan, Gary Paul. 1991. Restoring and Re-storying the Landscape. *Restoration and Management Notes* 9(1): 1–4. http://er.uwpress.org/content/9/1/3.full.pdf.

Sheridan, Thomas E., Nathan F. Sayre, and David Seibert. 2014. Beyond Stakeholders and the Zero Sum Game: Toward Community-Based Conservation in the West. In Susan Charnley, Thomas E. Sheridan, and Gary P. Nabhan, eds., *Stitching the West Back Together: Conservation of Working Landscapes* (pp. 53–75). University of Chicago Press, Chicago, IL.

Snyder, Gary. 1969. *Earth House Hold*. New Directions, San Francisco, CA.

Stevens, Sharon MacKenzie. 2007. *A Place for Dialogue: Language, Land Use and Politics in Southern Arizona*. University of Iowa, Iowa City, IA.

White, Courtney. 2014. The Quivira Experience: Reflections from a "Do": Tank. In Susan Charnley, Thomas E. Sheridan, and Gary P. Nabhan, eds., *Stitching the West Back Together: Conservation of Working Landscapes* (pp. 81–94). University of Chicago Press, Chicago, IL.

White, Courtney, et al. 2003. Invitation to the Radical Center. *Forging a West That Works.* http://www.awestthatworks.com.

Zayac, Sharon. 2003. The Earth Is Our Household. *Health Progress: Journal of the Catholic Health Association.* http://www.chausa.org/docs/default/health-progress/the-earth-is-our-household-pdf.

Chapter Three. Will Work for Dirt

Adi, S. 2016. Rhizosphere, Food Security, and Climate Change: A Critical Role for Plant-Soil Research. *Rhizosphere* 1: 1–3. https://doi.org/10.1016/j.rhisph.2016.08.005.

Ecker, Liz Slausson. 1990. *Population Enhancement of Rare Arizona Cactus,* Mammilaria thornberi *Orcutt (Cactaceae)* (MS thesis). Arizona State University, Tempe, AZ.

Gill, Charlotte. 2011. *Eating Dirt: Deep Forests, Big Timber, and Life with the Tree-Planting Tribe.* Greystone Books/D & M Publishers, Vancouver, British Columbia.

Intergovernmental Technical Panel on Soil Resources. 2015. *Status of the World's Soil Resources.* United Nations Food and Agriculture Organization, Rome, Italy.

Mahall, B. E., and R. M. Callaway. 1992. Root Communication Mechanisms and Intracommunity Distributions of Two Mojave Desert Shrubs. *Ecology* 73: 2145–2151. doi: 10.2307/1941462.

Marquardt, Jessica. 2016. Personal communication to Nabhan from ReNature, Tempe, AZ.

Martinez, Theodore N., and Nancy Collins Johnson. 2010. Agricultural Management Influences Propagule Densities and Functioning of Arbuscular Mycorrhizas in Low- and High-Input Agroecosystems in Arid Environments. *Applied Soil Ecology* 46: 300–306.

Mills, Jacob C., Phillip Weinstein, Nicholas J. C. Gellie, Laura S. Weyrich, Andrew J. Lowe, and Martin F. Breed. 2017. Urban Habitat Restoration Provides a Human Health Benefit through Microbial Rewilding: The Microbiomes Rewilding Hypothesis. *Restoration Ecology* 25(6): 866–872.

Rossiter, David G. 2007. Classification of Urban and Industrial Soils in the World Reference Base for Soil Resources. *Journal of Soils and Sediments*: 1–5. doi: http://dx.doi.org/10.1065/jss2007.02.208.

Sampson, R. Neil. 1981. *Farmland or Wasteland: A Time to Choose*. Rodale Press, Emmaus, PA.

Scheer, Rodney, and Doug Moss. 2013. Dirt Poor: Have Fruits and Vegetables Become Less Nutritious? *Scientific American*. http://www.scientificamerican .com/article/soil-depletion-and-nutrition-loss. Quoting Gabe Brown and *British Food Journal*.

Simard, S. W., Kevin J. Beiler, Marcus A. Bingham, Julie R. Deslippe, Leanne J. Philip, and François P. Teste. 2012. Mycorrhizal Networks: Mechanisms, Ecology and Modeling. *Fungal Biology Reviews* 26: 39–60.

USDA Natural Resource Conservation Service. 2007. *Soil Erosion on Cropland 2007*. http://www.nrcs.usda.gov/wps/portal/nrcs/detail.

Chapter Four. Replenishing Water and Wealth

Bank, David. 2014, September 19. Beartooth Capital: Conserving Wide Open Spaces. *ImpactAlpha*. Case Foundation, Washington, DC.

Daggett, Dan, and Jay Dusard. 1995. *Beyond the Rangeland Conflict: Toward a West That Works*. Quarto Press, Layton, UT.

Nabhan, Gary Paul. 2014. Healing the Lands of the Border: Joe Quiroga. *Land Conservation and Advocacy Trust*. Framingham, MA. http://www.lcatrust.org.

Nabhan, Gary Paul, Laura Lopez Hoffman, Hanna Gosnell, Josh Goldstein, Richard Knight, Carrie Presnall, Lauren Gwin, Dawn Thilmany, and Susan Charnley. 2014. Payment for Ecosystems Services: Keeping Working Landscapes Productive and Functioning. In Susan Charnley, Thomas E. Sheridan, and Gary P. Nabhan, eds., *Stitching the West Back Together: Conservation of Working Landscapes* (pp. 275–294). University of Chicago Press, Chicago, IL.

Norman, Laura, et al. 2015. Hydrologic Response of Streams Restored with Check Dams in the Chiricahua Mountains, Arizona. *River Research and Applications* 283: 1535–1567. https://DOI.org/10.10002/RA.2895.

Norman, Laura, and Rewati Niraula. 2016. Model Analysis of Check Dam Impacts on Long-Term Sediment and Water Budgets in Southeastern Arizona USA. *Ecohydrology and Hydrobiology* 16(3): 125–133.

Chapter Five. Bringing Back the Bison

Camp, Martha. 2009. *Thunder Heart Bison*. Heritage Network Radio. Atlanta, GA.

Chotzinoff, Robin. 2009. Honoring the Animal. *Edible Austin*. https://www.edibleaustin.org.

Fitzsmons, Hugh. 2018. *A Rock between Two Rivers*. Trinity University Press, San Antonio, TX.

Lott, Dale F. 2002. *American Bison: A Natural History*. University of California Press, Berkeley, CA.

Meinzer, Weiman, and Andrew Samson. 2011. *Southern Plains Bison: Resurrection of a Lost Texas Herd*. Badlands Blue Star Publications, Benjamin, TX.

Nabhan, Gary Paul, Deja Walker, and Alberto Mellado Moreno. 2010. Biocultural and Ecogastronomic Restoration: The Renewing America's Food Traditions Alliance. *Ecological Restoration*, 28(3), 266-279.

Chapter Six. Teach a Community to Fish

Cob, Jonathan Nathan. 1899. *The Sturgeon Fisheries of Delaware River and Bay*. US Fish Commission, Washington, DC.

Garret, Gary P. 2002. Community Involvement: A More Comprehensive Approach to Recovering Endangered Species. In *Conference Proceedings: Spring-Fed Wetlands: Important Scientific and Comprehensive Resources of the Intermountain Region*. Desert Research Institute. Paradise, NV.

Hale, Edward A., Ian A. Park, Matthew T. Fisher, Richard A. Wong, Michael J. Strangl, and John H. Clark. 2016. Abundance Estimate for and Habitat Use by Early Juvenile Atlantic Sturgeon with the Delaware River Estuary. *Transactions of the American Fisheries Society* 145(6): 1193–1201.

Hulazakim, Tim, and Leo G. Waisbey. 2004. Native American Utilization of Sturgeon. In G. T. O. Breton, F. W. Beamish, and S. R. McKinley, eds., *Sturgeons and Paddlefish of North America*. SpringerLink, NY.

Murray, Molly. 2016, June 5. Rebuilding Sturgeon Numbers in the Delaware River. *News Journal*. https://www.delawareonline.com/story/news/local/2016/06/05/rebuilding-sturgeon-numbers-delaware/85356560/.

Smith, T. I. J., and J. P. Clugston. Status and Management of Atlantic Sturgeon. Environmental Biology of Fishes. In V. J. Birstein, J. R. Walden, and W. E. Bemis, eds., *Developments in Sturgeon Biology and Conservation* (pp. 335–346). SpringerLink, NY.

Van Rossum, Maya. 2012, January 2. The Atlantic Sturgeon (*Acipenser oxyrinchus*) of the Delaware River—a Story of Plenty and Decline. *Delaware Riverkeeper.* http://www.delawareriverkeeper.org/ongoing-issues/atlantic-sturgeon.

Walsh, Stephen J., Howard L. Jelks, and Noel M. Burkhead. 2017. The Decline of North American Freshwater Fishes. *Action BioScience.* http://www.actionbioscience.org/biodiversity/walsh.html.

Williams, Ted. 2015. Atlantic Sturgeon: An Ancient Fish Struggles against the Flow. *Yale Environment* 420.

Chapter Seven. Plant Midwives

Barsh, Russell, and Madrona Murphy. 2016. Coast Salish Camas Cultivation. *HistoryLink.org* essay 11220. http://www.historylink.org/File/1200.

Davis-Hollander, Lawrence. 2008. Ramps (Wild Leeks): When Is Local Not Kosher? *grit.com.* https://www.grit.com/food/ramps-wild-leeks.

Kerr, Christel C., Laura S. Kenefic, and Susan L. Stout. 2015. Bridging the Gender Gap: The Demographics of Scientists in the USDA Forest Service and Academia. *BioScience* 65: 1165–1172.

Kimmerer, Robin. 2011. Restoration and Reciprocity: The Contributions of Traditional Ecological Knowledge. In D. Egan, E. E. Hjerpe, and J. Abrams, eds., *Human Dimensions of Ecological Restoration: Integrating Science, Nature and Culture* (pp. 257–276). Island Press, Washington, DC.

Kuzivanova, Valeria. 2016. *Restoring Manomin (Wild Rice): A Case Study with Wabaseemoong Independent Nations* (MS thesis). University of Manitoba, Winnipeg, Canada.

Kuzivanova, Valeria, and Iain J. Davidson-Hunt. 2017. Biocultural Design: Harvesting Manomin with Wabaseemoong Independent Nations. *Journal of Ethnobiology* 8(1): 794.

Nabhan, Gary Paul, and Rose Houk. 2004. Modern Day Hunters and Gatherers: Community Wild Foraging Project. In Peter Friederici and Rose Houk, eds., *A New Plateau: Sustaining the Lands and Peoples of Canyon Country* (pp. 90–95). Renewing the Countryside Publishing, Minneapolis, MN. http://www.renewingthecountryside.org/.

Senapril, Indrani. 2008, April 19. When Digging for Ramps Goes Too Deep. *New York Times.* http://www.nytimes.com/2011/04/20/dining/20forage.html.

Wagner, Eric. 2012, August 15. In Search of Camas, a Native American Food Staple. *High Country News* 44(13). http://www.hcn.org/issues/44.13.

West, Patty, Teresa DeKoker, and Susie Kovacs, with Gary Paul Nabhan. 2004. *Community-Based Wild Foraging: A Guide.* Center for Sustainable Environments, Northern Arizona University, Flagstaff, AZ.

World Ban. 2010. *Gender and Natural Resources Management Module 10: Overview.* World Bank, New York, NY. http//www.documents/worldbank.org.

Chapter Eight. Strange Birds Flock Together

Chrisman, Carolyn J., and Robert O. Hawes. 1999. *Birds of a Feather: Saving Rare Turkeys from Extinction.* American Livestock Breeds Conservancy, Pittsboro, NC.

Martin, A., D. P. Sponenberg, and J. Beranger. 2016. *Counting Our Chickens—the Great American Poultry Census.* The Livestock Conservancy, Pittsboro, NC.

Nabhan, Gary Paul, ed. 2014. *Conservation You Can Taste: Best Practices in Heritage Food Recovery and Successes in Restoring Agricultural Biodiversity of the Last Quarter Century.* Slow Food USA and University of Arizona Southwest Center, Tucson, AZ.

Waldkoenig, Gilson A. C. 2015. Ecological Restoration and Scenes of Grace. *Journal of Lutheran Ethics.* http://www.elca.org/JLE/Articles/1073.

Chapter Nine. Herders of Many Cultures

Anonymous. 2010. Mera Declaration of the Global Gathering of Women Pastoralists. *International Land Coalition.* http://www.landcoalition.org/en/news/mera-declaration-global-gathering-women-pastoralists.

Capalbo, Carla. 2015, December 23. The Fight to Preserve Traditional Pastureland. *Zester Daily.* http://zesterdaily.com/agriculture/fight-preserve-traditional-pastureland/.

Human, Katy. 2007, May 7. Churro Project Studies Rugged Sheep. *Denver Post.* http://www.denverpost.com/2005/05/07/churro-project-studies-rugged-desert-sheep/.

Nabhan, Gary Paul. 2006. *The Return of the Navajo-Churro Sheep.* Northern Arizona Center for Sustainable Environments. Flagstaff, AZ.

Upton, Caroline. 2014. The New Politics of Pastoralism: Identity, Justice and Global Activism. *Geoforum* 54: 207–216. http://www.sciencedirect.com/science/journal/00167185/54/supp/C54.

Chapter Ten. Immigrant Grains

Chamberlain, Chris. 2015, April 6. Anson Mills Boss Glenn Roberts Is the Guy to Know for Heirloom Grains in America. Southern Grown Series. *Food Republic.com.*

Kimble, Megan. 2015. It's Not about the Bread. *Edible Baja Arizona Magazine.* http://www.ediblebajaarizona.com/its-not-about-the-bread-html. Reprinted in *Best Food Writing of 2015.*

Moerman, Daniel E. 1998. *Native American Ethnobotany.* Timber Press, Portland, OR.

Nabhan, Gary Paul. 2011. *Heritage Grains of the Desert Borderlands: Their Return to the Santa Cruz River Valley and to Your Table.* Western SARE/ Native Seeds/SEARCH, Tucson, AZ.

Nabhan, Gary Paul. 2012. The Rising of White Sonora Wheat: Reviving the Best and Oldest Cake Flour in North America. *Heirloom Gardener Magazine,* fall: 60–63.

Neimark, Jill. 2017, May 10. A Lost Rice Variety—and the Story of the Freed "Merikans" Who Kept It Alive. *National Public Radio.*

Pandolfi. Keith. 2016, May. The Story of Carolina Gold, the Best Rice You've Never Tasted. *Serious Eats.* http://www.seriouseats.com/2016/05/Carolina -Gold-heirloom-rice-Ansoin-Mills.html.

Schulze, Richard. 2005. *Carolina God Rice: The Ebb and Flow History of a Lowcountry Cash Crop.* The History Press, Charleston, SC.

Shields, David. 2015. *Southern Provisions: The Creation and Revival of a Cuisine.* University of Chicago Press, Chicago, IL.

Chapter Eleven. Urban Growers and Rare Fruits

Crawford, Amy. 2012, January 4. Renegade Arborists Creating Forbidden Fruit in San Francisco. *San Francisco Examiner.* http://www.sfexaminer.com/ sanfrancisco/renegade-arborists-creating-forbidden-fruit-in-san-francisco/ Content?oid=2189270.

D'Andres, Nick. 2010, December 22. The Mysterious Date Palms of Phoenix. *Phoenix New Times.* http://www.phoenixnewtimes.com/arts/the-mysterious -date-palms-of-phoenix-6582888.

Jacobsen, Rowan. 2014. *Apples of Uncommon Character: 123 Heirlooms, Modern Classics and Little-Known Wonders.* Bloomsbury Books, New York, NY.

Nabhan, Gary Paul, ed. 2008. *Renewing America's Food Traditions: Saving and Savoring the Continent's Most Endangered Foods*. Chelsea Green Press, White River Junction, VT.

Nabhan, Gary Paul. 2010. A Fig by Any Other Name. *Gastronomica: Journal of Gastronomic Studies* 10(3): 15–18. https://www.garynabhan.com/news/2010/08/a-fig-by-any-other-name.html.

Nabhan, Gary Paul. 2013, November 1. Nomadic Nurseries, Guerrilla Grafters, and SNAP Seed Sowers: How Food Biodiversity Can Help the Poor in Our Communities. *Edible Baja Arizona*. http://ediblebajaarizona.com/nomadic-nurseries-guerrilla-grafters-and-snap-seed-sowers.html.

Ostrander, Matthew. 2017, November. The Old Adventures of the Newtown Pippin Apples. *Hard Cider Reviews*: 15. http://hardciderreviews.com/the-old-adventures-of-newtown-pippin-apples/.

Philander, Lisa, Kanin Josef Routson, and Rafael Routson de Grenade. 2010. Black Sphinx Date Palm (Unpublished research paper/powerpoint). University of Arizona School of Geography and Regional Development, Tucson, AZ.

Randazzo, Ryan. 2010, December 29. SRP, Phoenix Neighborhoods Find Palm Tree Solution. *Arizona Republic*. http://www.azcentral.com.

Seed Savers Exchange, ed. 2015. *Nursery Trade Catalog: Directory of Commercial Fruits, Berries and Nuts in the United States*. Seed Savers Exchange, Decorah, IA.

Chapter Twelve. Return of the Pollinators

Allen-Wardell, G., P. Bernhardt, R. Bitner, A. Burquez, S. Buchmann, J. Cane, P. Cox, V. Dalton, P. Feinsinger, M. Ingram, D. Inouye, C. Jones, K. Kennedy, P. Kevan, H. Koopowitz, R. Medellin, S. Medellin-Morales, G. Nabhan, B. Pavlik, V. Tepedino, P. Torchio, and S. Walker. 1998. The Potential Consequences of Pollinator Declines on the Conservation of Biodiversity and Stability of Food Crop Yields. *Conservation Biology* 12(1): 8–17.

Buchmann, Stephen, and Gary Paul Nabhan. 1996. *The Forgotten Pollinators*. Island Press, Washington, DC.

Buckley, Steve, and Gary Paul Nabhan. 2016. Food Chain Restoration for Pollinators. *Natural Areas Journal* 36(4): 489–497.

Castillo, Fernando. 2017, December 22. El murcielago mexicano es responable de la rica cultura del agave en Mexico. *CC News*. http://www.culturacolectiva.com/medio-ambiente/murcielago-mexicano.htpl.

Fleming, Theodore. 2004. Nectar Corridors: Migration and the Annual Cycle of Lesser Long-Nosed Bats. In Gary Paul Nabhan, ed., *Conserving Migratory Pollinators and Nectar Corridors in Western North America* (pp. 23–42). University of Arizona Press and Arizona-Sonora Desert Museum, Tucson, AZ.

Medellin, Rodrigo A., J. Guillermo Tellez, and Joaquin Arroyo. 2004. Conservation through Research and Education: An Example of Collaborative Integral Actions for Migratory Bats. In Gary Paul Nabhan, ed., *Conserving Migratory Pollinators and Nectar Corridors in Western North America* (pp. 43–58). University of Arizona Press and Arizona-Sonora Desert Museum, Tucson, AZ.

Nabhan, Gary Paul. 2012. *On Farm Habitat: Project Overview FW12-068*. https://projects.sare.org/sare_PROJECT/fw12-068/.

National Research Council. 2007. *Status of Pollinators in North America*. The National Academics Press, Washington, DC.

Rogers, Shelley R., David R. Tarpy, and Hannah J. Burrack. 2014. Bee Species Diversity Enhances Productivity and Stability in a Perennial Crop. *PLOS ONE* 9(5): 1–8.

Stein, Katharina, Drissa Coulibay, Kathrin Staenchly, Dethardt Goetze, Stefan Poremski, Andre Lindner, Souleymane Konate, and Eduard K. Linsemair. 2017. Bee Pollination Increases Yield Quantity and Quality of Cash Crops in Burkina Faso, West Africa. *Scientific Reports* 7(17,691). http://www.nature.com/scientificreports.

Tepedino, Vince J., and H. S. Ginzberg, eds. 2000. *Report of the US Department of Agriculture and US Department of Interior Joint Workshop on Declining Pollinators*. USGS/BRD/ITR 2000-007. Patuxent Wildlife Research Center, Patuxent, MD.

Withgott, Jay. 1999. Pollination Migrates to the Top of the Conservation Agenda. *BioScience* 49: 857–862.

Chapter Thirteen. You Can Go Home Again

Di Giovine, M. A., Jonathan Mabry, and T. Majewski. 2017. Moveable Feasts: Food as Revitalizing Cultural Heritage. In H. Silverman, E. Waterton, and S. Watson, eds., *Heritage in Action*. Springer, Cham.

Mabry, Jonathan, Gary Paul Nabhan, and Robert Ojeda. 2016. *State of Tucson's Food System, 2015–2016*. University of Arizona and Tucson Mayor's Food Commission on Food Security, Heritage and Economy, Tucson, AZ.

Nabhan, Gary Paul. 2017. Food, Community, Justice. *Slow Money Journal* 2016/2017: 91–101.

Nabhan, Gary Paul, and Jonathan Mabry. 2017. Food from Somewhere: The Power of Place-Based Labeling to Support Local Food Economies. *Edible Baja Arizona*. http://ediblebajaarizona.com/food-from-somewhere.

Nabhan, Gary Paul, Jonathan Mabry, Danielle Johnson, and Carolina Ferrales. 2017. *Pioneering Affordable Access to Food Biodiversity in Tucson, Arizona, a UNESCO City of Gastronomy*. State of Tucson's Food System, 2017–2018. University of Arizona and Tucson City of Gastronomy, Tucson, AZ.

Newman, Dennis. 2017. Gateway Gardening. *Edible Baja Arizona* 26: 86–92. http://ediblebajaarizona.com/gateway-gardening.

Nock, Magdalena Barros. 2009. Swap Meets and Socioeconomic Alternatives for Mexican Immigrants: The Case of San Joaquin Valley. *Human Organization* 68(3): 307–317.

US Census Bureau. 2017. American Community Survey. https://www.census .gov/programs-surveys/acs/.

Index

Island Press | Board of Directors

Pamela Murphy
(Chair)

Terry Gamble Boyer
(Vice Chair)
Author

Tony Everett
(Treasurer)
Founder, Hamill, Thursam
& Everett

Deborah Wiley
(Secretary)
Chair, Wiley Foundation, Inc.

Decker Anstrom
Board of Directors,
Discovery Communications

Melissa Shackleton Dann
Managing Director,
Endurance Consulting

Margot Ernst

Alison Greenberg
Executive Director,
Georgetown Heritage

Marsha Maytum
Principal,
Leddy Maytum Stacy Architects

David Miller
President, Island Press

Georgia Nassikas
Artist

Alison Sant
Co-Founder and Partner,
Studio for Urban Projects

Ron Sims
Former Deputy Secretary,
U.S. Department of Housing
and Urban Development

Sandra E. Taylor
CEO, Sustainable Business
International LLC

Anthony A. Williams
CEO & Executive Director,
Federal City Council